"Jesus calls His disciples to be attempt to integrate Jesus's call to 'followship' with the world's desire to use power and control from a position of leadership. Mark David Cooper argues that something similar has happened with baptism. Although Christian traditions agree that salvation is by grace alone through faith alone in Christ alone, they tend to integrate a long list of works into the process of growth in godliness. Water baptism is often one of those works. Some require baptism for church membership. Many require a particular mode of baptism at a specific time. Others require rebaptism if those requirements are not met. How did the gracious gift of God turn into a set of practices demanded of Christ's followers?

"From a study of the ways *baptism* is used in Scripture, Cooper argues that the major focus in the Bible is on *Baptism of Grace* wherein God immerses His people in His grace. Thus, the focus should be on the gracious gift we have received rather than on a human work performed in, with, or by water. Although many Christians will continue to see the value and purpose of baptism in water, Cooper helpfully calls attention back to the gracious gift from a gracious God. Instead of arguments about how much water and the mode of application, Christians can rest in the grace they have received from the God who loves them with a pure and holy love."

—**Glenn R. Kreider, PhD**,
Editor in Chief of *Bibliotheca Sacra*,
Acting Chair and Professor of Theological Studies,
Dallas Theological Seminary

"*Baptism of Grace* is an excellent read with beautiful biblical references that helped me better understand God's grace and love for all believers. I was taught at an early age, having been baptized as an infant, that this act was the only way to be saved. I often worried about friends who were believers but had not been baptized and did not practice going to church. The biblical references shared show 'the only requirement to be His disciple is to follow Him.' God understands our struggles and accepts us for who we are, the wonderful love of His grace!"

—Bob R. Tergerson,
Retired Director of Operations,
Quest Diagnostics

"*Baptism of Grace* is a well-thought-out treatise on the essential baptisms for Christians, helping all to understand the need for each baptism. Mark has thoroughly researched the six baptisms, bringing all of them to prominence. The *Baptism of Grace* is often ignored, just passed over without giving it a thought, but God's grace is essential for each of us to understand and appropriate. Do not shortchange grace in your walk with the Lord!"

—Rev. William Morford,
Editor, *One New Man Bible* translation,
Translator, *The Power New Testament*,
Author of *God's Rhythm of Life*, *This God We Serve*,
One New Man Bible Companion Volumes I, II, III, and *IV,* and
Myths of the Bible

Baptism of Grace

Mark David Cooper

Founder and President of *justBible Ministries*

CLAY BRIDGES
PRESS

Baptism of Grace

Mark David Cooper
Founder and President of *justBible Ministries*

For information about *justBible Ministries*:
http://justbibleministries.org/index.html
jbm.ministries@justbibleministries.org

Front cover image design by Lisa M. Robertson, Instagram @lisarobertsonart, lisarobertsonart.com, Lisarobertsonart@gmail.com

ISBN 978-1-953300-66-9 (paperback)
ISBN 978-1-953300-65-2 (ebook)

Special Sales: Most Clay Bridges titles are available in special quantity discounts. Custom imprinting or excerpting can also be done to fit special needs. For standard bulk orders, go to www.claybridgesbulk.com. For specialty press or large orders, contact Clay Bridges at info@claybridgespress.com.

Table of Contents

Thank You To

My God for revealing this message to me through studying Your Word.

Pamela Cooper for your support, encouragement, edits, and feedback, and for being my wife.

Lisa Robertson for using God's gift to design the book cover image.

Everyone (domestic United States and international) who participated in symposiums, Bible studies, and discussions that helped me hone this message from God.

Introduction

It is hard to understand the magnitude of God's grace, which is unfathomable and impossible to comprehend. As a failed and sinful human, how can a God who is perfect and holy love us enough to save us from our willful disobedience and astoundingly continue loving us as we stumble though this life? In our guilt of previous failures, struggling faith, and physical frailty, God loves us and uses us. It is hard to understand.

The Apostle Paul dealt with the same issue and documented it in his second letter to the believers in Corinth (2 Cor. 12). Paul had a condition that haunted him. We do not have the specific details on what bothered him, but we do know that he pleaded to God to take it away. There are many theories about what afflicted Paul. One thought is that it was a physical condition, and another is that he suffered from the guilt of his past persecution of the followers of Jesus before the road to Damascus event in Acts 9. Regardless of what this affliction was, Paul pleads, and God responds, "My grace is sufficient for you, for power is perfected in weakness" (2 Cor. 12:9). Because of God's grace, Paul proclaims the crucified Christ as the Son of God and Savior, and people are reading and studying his writings thousands of years later.

Every person struggles. Regardless of our size, shape, color, economic status, education, position, physical condition, emotional condition, or spiritual position, we all struggle. All of us have something in our life we would love God to remove. It might be guilt, it might be addiction, it might be loneliness, it might be sadness, it might be a loss, or it might be fear. The list goes on and on. What we must understand is that everyone struggles. No one is unaccompanied in their struggle. God says to you today, "My grace is sufficient for you, for power is perfected in weakness." What God says is that what we suffer from is the very thing that will show us His love, power, and glory. This grace is beyond our capability to understand. What we think of as a deterrent, what we believe disqualifies us, what the world says is worthless, God says that He will make those conditions the strength of our witness and the source of proclaiming Jesus Christ. What we can understand is our inadequacies and failures. This comprehension and the knowledge that God completely covers, eliminates, and forgets our human, sinful condition show us a glimpse of His grace.

After a lucrative career in a major corporation and working for a major nonprofit, I started a ministry to fulfill the Lord's command of making disciples. The endless efforts of fundraising, developing teaching notebooks, fundraising, scheduling, planning international symposiums, fundraising, managing multiple international projects, fundraising, providing funds for international partners, fundraising, writing thank-you letters and annual reports, fundraising, prioritizing where donated funds are sent, fundraising, traveling internationally, and receiving numerous daily requests for funds accumulated into an overwhelming burden. The burden was so great that I started wondering where God was in all of this. Resentment, discouragement, and anger started taking over my thoughts.

I left the house at 6:30 a.m. every morning to work at a parttime job because I chose to not take a salary from the ministry. The international partners were not working and continually asked for more and more money. I gave up a career for the Lord, and I expected Him to make doing ministry easy. I pleaded to God for help. I asked Him to provide something or someone to come alongside the ministry and help with the overwhelming burden of fundraising and administration. But those requests were not fulfilled.

God, where are you? I have done my part. I have done what You asked. I have given it all up for You. I have put in my best, yet all I am sensing is silence from You. God, where are You? I quoted His promises back to Him: "I will never desert you, nor will I ever forsake you" (Heb. 13:5), "My yoke is easy and My burden is light" (Matt. 11:30), "Commit your works to the LORD and your plans will be established" (Prov. 16:3). And yet I hit the wall. The discouragement and lack of answered prayers were overwhelming. God, where are You? It was then that I realized I needed to step back and do a personal assessment. I had to ask who God is and what He wants from me. I had to go back to the basics of faith.

Just like Job, I attempted to intimidate and challenge God. I needed to understand who I am and who God is. So I read God's response to Job when he challenged and questioned God. Job suffered greatly and experienced economic loss, business loss, family loss, sickness, excommunication, and judgment by his friends. As any of us would react, Job challenged God. Job complained. Job asked questions. Job sought advice. Eventually,

God answered (Job 38–42). In a magnificent way, God addressed Job and explained that He is the supreme Creator of everything, from the control of the ocean shores to how and when a horse gives birth. God never addressed Job's problems. God did not confirm to Job that his situation was terrible. In a direct pontification, God explained that humanity has no right to challenge, question, or complain about what He is doing. Job's only response can be paraphrased as, "I am nothing compared to the Lord." And so my response also had to be, "I am nothing compared to the Creator, the Sovereign Lord."

Do you need to step back and bring your faith back to the basics? Do you need to say to the Lord, "I am nothing compared to the Creator, the Sovereign Lord"? From time to time, we all need to reset our faith and remember that the narrative of life is a reconciliation with our Creator. The first step is recognizing who He is, what He has done for us, and what He promises. It is only then that we can obtain a clear picture of His grace and continue maturing our faith and study the depths of His Word.

And what about my question: "Where are You, Lord?" Paul's message in Athens when he addressed the statue of the unknown God answers that question. God is in our breath, life, and being (Acts 17:22–31). Understanding that God is the source of our breath answers where He is. The fact that we breathe is indication enough that God is present. Breathing is a function we do not think about until it becomes hindered.

While waking up after a minor surgery where the doctors pumped a lot of air into my body, causing my lungs to be compressed, I was struggling to breathe. I remember fighting and struggling, mightily gasping for air. Those who have experienced the challenge of breathing understand the value of a good intake of air. Each breath we take is an indication of God's presence.

When we ask, "Where are You, God?" it is like we lost our ability to breathe. What we are really doing is not questioning His existence or denying that He loves us. We are fighting and grasping for His sustaining grace and presence. The realization of basic faith is that God is God and in control. Our breathing is the indicator of His presence, and His grace is sufficient.

Is it that simple? Can it be that simple? Do we accept that simplistic faith?

We struggle because we want to add to the simplicity of faith. We need something more physical, and we want to work to achieve faith. We add disciplines when all God asks us to do is "Cease *striving* and know that I am God" (Ps. 46:10). But we want to toil, stress, strive, run after, be successful, build, and pursue. God says, "Breathe, and know that I am God" (my paraphrase). We have a deep remorse for our rebellion against God, so we seek to appease His wrath. Even though we understand that Christ paid the debt, we still long to pay penitence for our failures. God says, "My grace is sufficient."

Do we really understand this grace? Paul even struggled with it.

The church institution (what society calls the church today) contributes to the psyche of having to do *something* in addition to the acknowledgment that Christ the Messiah saved and covered our sins. Here are just a few of those have-tos:

- Raise your hand to accept Jesus.
- Come on down to the front and make a public confession.
- Pray the sinner's prayer.
- Go to a priest, and confess your sins.
- Attend a service or mass every week.
- Recount daily if you committed any of the seven deadly sins.

- Pray every night for forgiveness for the sins you *might* have committed.
- Attend a new members' class.
- Become a member.
- *Be baptized!*

All these are legalistic, human-generated requirements to keep people oppressed and in subjection to human authority. When our Messiah Jesus Christ died on the cross, *all* the earthly, physical, legalistic action requirements were eliminated. The Word of God teaches that because of Christ's sacrifice, we who believe have freedom and a direct relationship with the Father that is guided by the Holy Spirit. Our challenge today is to step back from what the church institution teaches and embrace the liberty that the age of grace we live in offers. Baptism throughout history has been and is a detriment to this liberty, and we need to evaluate what it really means and what it is.

"Why does a person have to be immersed in water, and what is the necessity for baptism?" I asked the church elder who was teaching the new members' class. His face turned red, and his eyes were full of rage as he hit his fist on the table, pointed his finger at me, and said, "You *have* to be baptized (he meant the physical act of immersion in water) because it is being obedient to Jesus!" The tone of the membership class became even more tense when I asked, "Where does Jesus give this command?" He stumbled and referenced Matthew 28:19. I asked him to quote that verse for me, which he did. I then asked him, "Where in this verse is the command to be immersed in water? Where is water referenced? Was this statement in the original text?" His rage escalated, and he responded, "Jesus was baptized by being immersed in the river Jordan, so we have to follow His example and also be baptized by immersion in water." (Pause) I asked myself if I should continue. I could not resist and felt compelled to at least probe the truth more. So I asked, "Because Jesus died on the cross for my sin, do I literally and physically need to die on the cross too? The Bible says that John baptized with water and Jesus baptizes with the Holy Spirit. Shouldn't you be teaching that we need Jesus's baptism of the Holy Spirit?" His response: none. And this elder of the church who was teaching this class closed his notes, said, "Class is over," and walked out.

When challenged to defend their position regarding an act associated with water, the church institutions often become defensive. Most of the time, staff members become angry, frustrated, and turn their backs on the dialogue. When I asked a pastor, "Is baptism necessary for salvation?" his answer was no. Then my follow-up question was "Why, then, do we need to perform a physical water act?" He got frustrated and responded, "Attend the baptism class," and the conversation ended.

People have been denied church membership because they did not feel led by the Lord to get rebaptized by immersion when their parents in full faith had them baptized as an infant. Many churches today fail to see the inconsistency of their messaging, an inconsistency that repulses intelligent people who choose not to attend an organization because of their belief in a human-distorted, doctrinally earthly, physical water event. Today's staunch position of the church institution regarding this water event is no different than the position of the church institution in the 1500s. Many people today are hurt, lost, and lonely and feel outcast because of the church's dogmatic positions on physical rituals. These rituals, specifically water baptism, have torn Christendom apart for centuries.

The topic of baptism is a very emotional one, steeped in tradition and not individually processed or thought through

7

by many people—people who have either put themselves in a teaching position or have been assigned to preach and teach, repeating what the church institution or denomination doctrine dictates them to say.

What is sad today is that there is limited ability for dialogue with pastors, elders, or staff. The Pharisees at least provided the opportunity for discussion as they listened to Jesus and Paul in the synagogue. Today, most pastors do not answer the phone, return calls, or respond to emails. They are unreachable. Many of them are guarded with armed security, adding to the isolation between them and the people who are seeking the truth. This alone shows us their hypocrisy. They would be the first to say they live like Christ, but Jesus did not have a bodyguard and was publicly accessible to the leper, the sick, the lame, the blind, the rich, the poor, the educated, the laborer, all ethnic groups, and all sinners, and then He was arrested and murdered. Paul was beaten multiple times for teaching about Christ. Jesus and Paul did not hide from the tough questions. They were not afraid of the people and had a passion for the truth to be presented and accepted.

Today's church institution is structured in complete contrast. Often the person behind the pulpit pontificates their biased, preconceived position based on a couple of verses without any questioning or rebuttal. If someone were to stand up during a Sunday morning service today and say, "Excuse me . . ." they would be treated as a threat and escorted out of the service. What a shame that our society allows this to happen and accepts it as the norm. Maybe that is why the church institution is suffering today and many young people are staying away because they do not have an opportunity to ask questions or have a dialogue.

The church institutions today keep records of people who attend their services and events. Everyone is classified as a visitor, regular attender, candidate for baptism, baptized (according to guidelines), or member. Nowhere in the Word of God does it talk about classifying people like this. In his writing to the church in Ephesus, Paul classified people in the church as apostles, prophets, evangelists, pastors, teachers, and saints working as a unified body following Jesus Christ the Son of God (Eph. 4:10–16). In Paul's letter to the church in Corinth, he explains that everyone is equal and that "circumcision is nothing, and uncircumcision is nothing, but *what matters is* the keeping of the commandments of God" (1 Cor. 7:19). In Galatians 3:28, Paul, in his argument against the Galatian Gentiles being circumcised, states that when we are in Christ, "there is neither Jew nor Greek, there is neither slave nor free man, there is neither male nor female; for you are all one in Christ Jesus."

Where is the list from the church institution showing who is making disciples and taking care of the poor? Those are the true commandments from God. Baptism is presented as matter-of-fact from the pulpit, and the new members' class does not allow for good, in-depth study, conversation, or dialogue. People who have immaturely believed human traditions, accepted denominational doctrines, and quoted the church line are influencing other people to participate in an earthly, physical action that only satisfies human requirements.

The elder of the church in the previous example failed to understand that I grew up in a conservative Baptist church and was water baptized by immersion at the age of 12, fully understanding what I was doing as a believing Christian and buying into the obedience charge. He never stopped to ask, he never got to know my background, and he never inquired where I was in my relationship with the Lord. His task was to teach the doctrine that would move me onto the membership list. What the elder also did not find out was that my wife was sprinkled as an infant because, in faith, her parents presented her before the Lord. She grew up in the church, graduated from a confirmation class, and knows the Bible very well. She has an undeniable faith demonstrated throughout her life of following Christ with compassion and encouragement gifted from the Holy Spirit.

When we moved to a new city years ago, we set out to find a church to attend, have fellowship with believers, and grow in the study of God's Word. One Sunday afternoon, a young couple from the church visited us at our home. After a good conversation getting to know them and discussing the church, the topic turned to baptism because it was important to this particular church. When they discovered that my wife, Pam, was not immersed as a believer, they told me we could go upstairs, and I could baptize her in the bathtub. *What?* Their visit was quickly terminated as I explained that the church they represented was not a place for us. This was an affirmation that people and the church institution are ignorant and blind when it comes to the topic of baptism.

You might be thinking, "My church would do a better job than that." Really? Try asking your pastor, elder, or person teaching the membership class the same questions. When you do challenge that person, ask them to support their answers with the entire Bible and not just select partial verses or any human-developed denominational doctrine.

We have all sat and listened to many sermons over the years where preachers contradict themselves in the same sermon. It is an easy detection, and you have heard it. It goes like this: "Your salvation is free. It is a free gift of God; you do not have to do anything to earn salvation. All you need to do is accept this gift, pray the prayer, repent, and you are saved." (more preaching) (10 minutes later): "You *must* be obedient and follow the Lord in the waters of baptism. Once you do that, you need to become a member of the church." The Holy Spirit in your life should scream, "But you just said that salvation is free and there is no need to do anything else."

There is a story of a frog in a pot of water. If you put the frog in a cold pot of water, the frog will float and enjoy the cool bath. When you put the pot on a stove, turn on the heat, and bring it to a boil, the frog will still float and enjoy the bath until it boils to death. A frog's body temperature will adapt to the water temperature and will never feel uncomfortable. The frog does not even know it is being boiled alive because it has become comfortable.

The church institution is doing the same thing. People sit in services that are contradictory, and they do not even process what is being said. It is because they hear the same Christian rhetoric all the time and just adapt to the programming. When I hear this contradiction, I want to scream, "Wake up, people! You are being deceived!" But instead, I have laid low, not wanting to create an uproar in the church. Well, the time has come to not be silent anymore.

For those reading this who have participated in being baptized with water and experienced a life change, this writing is not to discredit or minimize your experience. In fact, it is to enhance your experience by explaining the depth of what transpires and what the Lord has done and is doing on your Christian journey.

Realizing how volatile the subject of baptism can become, I started studying this topic by praying, attending seminary, reading multiple perspectives, discussing the topic with safe fellow believers, and teaching it to people groups who are true disciples of Christ struggling with the shallowness of the modern church institution and denominations. During this study, I came across a book by Harry Bultema, written in 1952 and published in 1955 by his son, Daniel Bultema. The book is called *The Bible and Baptism: A Re-Examination.* Let me summarize this great work. Pastor Bultema uses Hebrews, Ephesians 2, Colossians 2, and Galatians to support his thesis that the necessity of the earthly, physical water event action was blotted (abolished) because of the work Yeshua the Messiah did on the cross. This book has not found its way into mainstream Christendom. It is counter to the cultural teaching and oppressive position regarding the must-do physical water act position of the church institution and religious denominations. Pastor Bultema argues that the modern-day water event ritual was derived from the Apocryphal books, the Talmud, and the washing of the Pharisees that Jesus condemned in Mark 7:1–23 and Luke 11:37–41. Look at what Pastor Bultema wrote.

> *Strict orthodox and Talmudic Jews still regard the Netilat Tadajun, the washing of hands, as a most important ritual practice. On rising in the morning, before and after meals, before prayers, they religiously wash their hands. And all these endless rules and regulations, with conditions, arose not merely from the fear that they might touch a dead fly or any other dead insect, but they were motivated by a well nigh universal desire to do something for God by means of the most universal element, water. They called these washings baptisms.*[1]

My search for the truth resulted in discovering the fullness of what it means to be baptized of grace using the entirety of what

---

1. Harry Bultema, *The Bible and Baptism: A Re-Examination* (Muskegon, MI: Bultema Memorial Publication Society, 1955), 32.

the Bible teaches. When you read this work and study what the Bible communicates regarding the topic of baptism, the prayer is that the Lord will reveal to you His unfathomable (as Paul conveys) grace and the salvation into which He baptizes you.

Before we dive deeply into the subject of baptism, we need to address a significant attitude of society that the church institution has also adopted. It is the astounding topic of *leadership*. Our society today screams that everyone must be self-centered and make people follow you. This is in direct contradiction to what the Bible teaches and how God wants us to conduct our lives. As Christians, we sing that we will follow Jesus, but then we attend seminars, go to classes, and read books and websites on how to become great *leaders*. The church institution also promotes this worldly motive as pastors write books on leadership based on biblical texts.

At no time did Jesus tell His disciples to be leaders.

Jesus taught His disciples to follow Him and to serve. The reason for spending time on the topic of following is significant in order to have our hearts attentive to God's leading so we are open to the fullness of the *Baptism of Grace* discussion. The desire is for us to seek the Lord and what He is saying. That means we need to put away human teachings and focus on what God teaches. To achieve the heart condition that God wants, we must deny ourselves and not strive to be served first (the world's heart desire) but to be a servant (God's heart desire).

We need to follow the Lord, not people!

Followship

Follow Me, and I will make you fishers of men.

—Matt. 4:19

When Jesus approached His recruits for discipleship, His invitation was consistent: "Follow me." Even when the rich ruler asked how to enter the Kingdom of God, Jesus invited him to sell everything, give it to the poor, and "follow me" (Mark 10:21). The message is consistent throughout the Gospels. The Messiah's directive to everyone is "Follow me."

- Jesus said to Peter and Andrew, "Follow Me, and I will make you fishers of men" (Matt. 4:19).
- To the man who wanted to bury his father, Jesus said, "Follow Me, and allow the dead to bury their own dead" (Matt. 8:22).
- Jesus invites Matthew to give up collecting taxes and "Follow Me!" (Matt. 9:9).

- Jesus instructs the disciples, "And he who does not take his cross and follow after Me is not worthy of Me" (Matt. 10:38).
- Jesus spoke to the Pharisees, saying, "I am the Light of the world; he who follows Me will not walk in the darkness, but will have the Light of life" (John 8:12).
- Jesus said to the Jews in the temple, "My sheep hear My voice, and I know them, and they follow Me" (John 10:27).

The invitation Jesus made to everyone was the same. The only requirement to be His disciple is to follow Him!

Peter accepted the Lord's invitation to give up his fishing career and followed the Messiah. All was well and the task was clear until Jesus was put to death. Peter, being confused, feeling guilty of denying Jesus and maybe frustrated that things did not turn out like he planned, returned to his old life of fishing. One morning, Peter's discipleship was changed forever. After a long night of fishing, he and his partners had not caught a single fish, and in the morning, they encountered the resurrected Messiah on the shore of Galilee. Peter had to admit to the Lord that his idea and effort netted nothing.

Jesus instructed Peter to perform the task of fishing in a completely contradictory method from the norm and to cast the nets on the opposite side of the boat. It was only when Peter followed Jesus's instruction that the catch was substantial and overflowing. But the story does not end there. In the subsequent dialogue, Jesus asks Peter three times, "Do you love me?" Three times Peter answers yes. Each time Jesus responded, "Tend My sheep" (John 21:17). Jesus told Peter to feed them, take care of them, and nurture them. Peter was to teach and show the people how to live for Jesus. The last command Jesus gave Peter was to "follow Me" (John 21:15–22). The message is consistent. At the discipleship recruitment of Peter, Jesus said, "Follow Me." When it was time for Peter's independence, Jesus instructed him, "Follow Me." This message at the end of the Gospel of John directs believers to teach about Christ and follow Him. As believers, we are to follow Jesus and show other people how to follow Him. We are to feed His people by teaching them His Word. We are to direct people to seek the Lord's guidance. We are to show people how to learn the Lord's truths. We are to point people toward the Lord. We are to influence people to live their lives for the *one true Leader*.

This is the genesis of *Followship* defined like this:

Influencing others toward following the Lord God.

Do not call anyone a leader.

Our worldly culture today promotes leadership. Thousands of books have been written, formulas have been developed, businesses have been built, and seminars have been generated to give people tools and actions to become leaders. While there are good ideas and thoughts that come out of this leadership industry, the challenge is to understand how this concept fits into God's design for humanity and how it lines up with God's desire to recognize Him as Lord and worship only Him.

The definition of *lead* is "to be first."[1] By taking this root and applying it to *leadership*, the concept of the term means "to be firstship" (term generated to highlight a point). Our culture

1. "Lead," *Webster's New World Dictionary, Third College Edition* (New York: Simon & Schuster, 1988), 767.

economy uses the term *leadership*. This subliminally indicates that everyone should strive to be first. As humans, our instilled natural default is to be first (Gen. 3). Satan's temptation of Eve was to directly challenge God's sovereign position and entice her to take control of her own destiny—"Did God really say you would die? He (God) just wanted to keep you ignorant and not have the same knowledge that He has" (my paraphrase). The natural human passion is to be in charge, to know everything, to elevate ourselves above everyone, including God. By definition, that is what the world calls leadership. As humans, we fight with every fiber in our character to resist being a follower. We want to be in charge. We want firstship.

Jesus provides a very clear warning regarding the strife for leadership. After Jesus silenced the Pharisees and scribes, He turned to all those who were with Him and said this:

The scribes and the Pharisees have seated themselves in the chair of Moses; therefore all that they tell you, do and observe, but do not do according to their deeds; for they say things, and do not do them. They tie up heavy burdens and lay them on men's shoulders, but they themselves are unwilling to move them with so much as a finger. But they do all their deeds to be noticed by men; for they broaden their phylacteries and lengthen the tassels of their garments. They love the place of honor at banquets and the chief seats in the synagogues, and respectful greetings in the market places, and being called Rabbi by men. But do not be called Rabbi; for One is your Teacher, and you are all brothers. Do not call anyone on earth your father; for One is your Father, He who is in heaven.

Do not be called leaders; for One is your Leader, that is, Christ. But the greatest among you shall be your servant. Whoever exalts himself shall be humbled; and whoever humbles himself shall be exalted.

—Matt. 23:1–12

The scribes and Pharisees elevated themselves to a position of authority. They turned the position of communicating God's statutes, ordinances, and Law into a profit-gaining leadership profession. Jesus tells His people to not do what the scribes and Pharisees do. He says do not be called a leader!

The world's economy: leadership.

God's economy: Followship.

God's economy is different than the worldly culture. Jesus says we should not be like the world. Jesus warns in Matthew to not strive to be like the church officials who have elevated themselves to the position of leader. God's economy is for us to dedicate our lives to following the Lord and influencing people to follow Him.

The question is this: What does *Followship* look like? We live in a time of history when the Word of God is in written form called the Bible. *Followship* is the immersion into the Bible, learning daily from it, studying it, and integrating it into our lives. Matthew 11:29 documents Jesus telling us to take up His yoke (His teachings) and learn from Him. His Word teaches us and guides us. We need to seek His counsel and wisdom for direction in our lives. When we seek His kingdom, His rules, and His heart, we know how we are to conduct our actions. We then have a responsibility to influence everyone we encounter to seek the Lord's guidance and follow Him and not any human being.

Believers, our call is to follow the Lord. That means read, study, and know His Word. It means listen to the conviction and prompting of the Holy Spirit. It means personally discern the truth. As you read the following chapters on baptism, the task is to set aside any preconceived thoughts, ideas, or convictions, and follow the Lord's teachings. As a reader, you have the responsibility to discern what is right and what is from the Lord.

Followship: *Influencing people to follow the Lord.*

Can We Define Baptism?

There is one body and one Spirit, just as also you were called in one hope of your calling; one Lord, one faith, one baptism, one God and Father of all who is over all and through all and in all.

—Eph. 4:4–6

For by one Spirit we were all baptized into one body, whether Jews or Greeks, whether slaves or free, and we were all made to drink of one Spirit.

—1 Cor. 12:13

And in Him you were also circumcised with a circumcision made without hands, in the removal of the body of the flesh by the circumcision of Christ; having been buried with Him in baptism, in which you were also raised up with Him through faith in the working of God, who raised Him from the dead.

—Col. 2:11–12

There is one body of believers in Christ, one Spirit, and one baptism performed by the Lord. But what does that mean? The Bible is very clear on this truth, yet through the years, baptism has become a controversial topic. It is so controversial that the Christian church has divided into many beliefs, factions, and denominations because of rigid positioning on the understanding of baptism. Strong disagreements exist on the method, mode, and even the eligibility of recipients of baptism. Differences of opinion occur on whether the acceptable action is the complete body immersed in water or the head sprinkled with water. Heated arguments commence regarding the age and spiritual status of a person to be baptized. Rigid positions are held about the role of baptism in salvation. Is it required for salvation or not? These differences have predominately focused on an earthly, physical water event that our culture calls baptism. This event has been elevated in church institutions today as a necessity for membership or even to be considered a Christian.

In 1982, the Faith and Order Commission of the World Council of Churches met in Geneva, Switzerland, to continue the discussion on three topics: baptism, the Eucharist, and ministry. The Commission recognized the need for unity and anguished over the biblical concept of one baptism with an attempt to encourage all doctrinal disciplines to accept the others' position. Sadly, they were unsuccessful. Here is their commentary on the section that calls for unity:

> The inability of the churches mutually to recognize their various practices of baptism as sharing in the one baptism, and their actual dividedness in spite of mutual baptismal recognition, have given dramatic visibility to the broken witness of the Church. The

readiness of the churches in some places and times to
allow differences of sex, race, or social status to divide
the body of Christ has further called into question
genuine baptismal unity of the Christian community
(Gal. 3:27–28) and has seriously compromised its
witness. The need to recover baptismal unity is at
the heart of the ecumenical task as it is central for
the realization of genuine partnership within the
Christian communities.[1]

What a tragedy and how sad it is to think that this is not what God intended. God wants us to have unity and fellowship in love, which is more valuable than any physical ritual. He provides one baptism. What is this one baptism? In this book, I am proposing that the one baptism is the *Baptism of Grace*. There are five unique baptisms that are found in the Bible: water, Trinity, Holy Spirit, fire, and blood. In the Hebrew, the number *five* represents grace. This book will provide the biblical support for each of the five baptisms and then discuss the significance of the number *five* and how it represents God's grace.

The conclusion of this work is that God baptizes His
people with His grace, which is the one baptism the
Word of God communicates.

As believers, our main priority is to bring glory to our Creator. But when we fixate on a narrow view of an earthly,

---

1. World Council of Churches, "Baptism, Eucharist, and Ministry," in John H. Leith, ed., *Creeds of the Churches* (Louisville, KY: John Knox Press, 1982), 608–609.

physical activity and mandate a particular ritual in order to join a body of fellowship, the focus becomes a human action and not the loving grace of God the Father. Rigid dogmatic positions have been established on the topic of baptism. Various generated regulations and rituals for the method of a water event baptism have resulted in damaging controversial opinions and doctrines.

The intent of this book is not to discredit, deny, challenge, or argue for or against any religious institution's water event practices. For a person to follow through with any type of physical water practice, it must be between that individual and the Lord. If parents choose to have their babies sprinkled, that decision is between them and the Lord. For a person to become physically immersed in water when they become "of age," it must be a decision made between them and the Lord. For denominations and church institutions to have doctrines that require a specific mode of a physical water event, that position must be between them and the Lord. Here is my intent in writing about the *Baptism of Grace*:

1. To expand the understanding of the fullness of baptism beyond an earthly physical water act
2. To investigate a fresh view that baptism is much bigger and more comprehensive than a human-performed water event
3. To grasp that baptism is a function that the Lord does to us and for us

The intent is not to condemn or change anyone's belief or conviction of an earthly, physical water baptism event. The intent is to expand the common thinking beyond just that physical event. It is to refocus our attention from ourselves or an institution to expanding our understanding of what the Lord does and how vast His grace is toward us.

First, there needs to be an assessment of how the Lord encounters each individual. He deals with people individually and uniquely. There is not a single formula for how the Lord deals and interacts with humanity. God spoke to Moses through a burning bush (Exod. 3), He met Gideon in a wine press (Judges 6), He communicated to Daniel through dreams (Dan. 7–8), and He spoke to Balaam through a donkey (Num. 22). Paul was knocked off his horse and saw a bright light (Acts 9), and John had a vision while on the island of Patmos (Rev. 1:9–11). Jesus told the ruler to go sell everything, give it to the poor, and then follow Him (Luke 18:18–27). Peter was approached after a night of fishing (Matt. 4:18–20), and Matthew was sitting at his tax collector's table when Jesus came to him (Mark 2:14).

The Lord approaches, communicates, and deals with everyone uniquely and personally. How we come to know the Lord is a unique and beautiful testimony and should never be forced into a standard format or ritual. Everyone's decision to believe and their choice to follow the Lord are all different. Some of us have great testimonies of an instant understanding and a dramatic life change like Paul, while others testify that their understanding of the Lord required a longer process and some convincing like Moses and Jonah.

Humanity's job is to bring glory to the Lord, love Him, live a life that demonstrates His love, and teach His word (Matt. 22:37–39; 28:19). The hardest part for us as humans is to leave it at that. Our responsibility is simple, yet we tend to make it very complicated. Just like the Pharisees who kept adding rules, attempting to clarify what God meant by the Law, we also add rites, rituals, and sacraments to our religious beliefs. God's true intent for us is not to get hung up on the physical activity. His desire is for us to live in fellowship with Him and conduct our actions with purity in alignment with His statutes. Samuel communicates God's desire to Saul when he says, "Has the LORD as much delight in burnt offerings and sacrifices as in obeying the voice of the LORD? Behold, to obey is better than sacrifice, and to heed than the fat of rams" (1 Sam. 15:22). David understood this.

> *Sacrifice and meal offering You have not desired;*
> *My ears You have opened;*
> *Burnt offering and sin offering You have not required.*
> *Then I said, "Behold, I come;*
> *In the scroll of the book it is written of me.*
> *I delight to do Your will, O my God;*
> *Your Law is within my heart."*
>
> —Ps. 40:6–8

Look at David's plea for forgiveness.

> *For You do not delight in sacrifice, otherwise I would give it;*
> *You are not pleased with burnt offering.*
> *The sacrifices of God are a broken spirit;*
> *A broken and a contrite heart, O God, You will not despise.*
>
> —Ps. 51:16–17

Isaiah documents God's real desire.

> *"What are your multiplied sacrifices to Me?"*
> *Says the LORD.*
> *"I have had enough of burnt offerings of rams*

And the fat of fed cattle;
And I take no pleasure in the blood of bulls, lambs or goats.
When you come to appear before Me,
Who requires of you this trampling of My courts?
Bring your worthless offerings no longer,
Incense is an abomination to Me.
New moon and sabbath, the calling of assemblies—
I cannot endure iniquity and the solemn assembly.
I hate your new moon festivals and your appointed feasts,
They have become a burden to Me;
I am weary of bearing them.
So when you spread out your hands in prayer,
I will hide My eyes from you;
Yes, even though you multiply prayers,
I will not listen.
Your hands are covered with blood.

"Wash yourselves, make yourselves clean;
Remove the evil of your deeds from My sight.
Cease to do evil,
Learn to do good;
Seek justice,
Reprove the ruthless,
Defend the orphan,
Plead for the widow."

—Isa. 1:11–17

Micah 6:6–8 states that doing justice, loving kindness, and walking humbly with God are more important than multitudes of calves, rams, or oil sacrifices. Hebrews 10:4–8 reiterates Psalm 40, explaining that the blood of bulls and goats cannot take away sins and that God does not delight in sacrifices. Paul uses circumcision as an illustration to communicate the concept of heart motive and condition versus a physical action. "And in Him you were also circumcised with a circumcision made without hands, in the removal of the body of the flesh by the circumcision of Christ" (Col. 2:11). It is consistent throughout the Word of God that our relationship with Him is predicated on a repentant and humble demeanor, a contrite attitude, and an alignment of motives that matches His compassion for people. To put this in terms we understand today, God could care less about all the earthly, physical rituals we perform, the programs we create, or the buildings we erect. All He wants is for us to have a heart that loves Him, loves people (Luke 10:27), and follows Him.

The *Baptism of Grace* challenges the reader to investigate the larger view of what the entire Word of God teaches about baptism. A deeper, more complex, and broader perspective of the concept of baptism beyond our current culture's understanding and teaching of a simple water event ritual is required to fully understand God's intention for relationship with believers. To fully grasp the *Baptism of Grace* concept, it is necessary that all presuppositions (past understandings, teachings, beliefs, experiences, and judgments) be set aside to contemplate new thoughts specifically regarding this controversial topic of baptism. Paul teaches in Galatians 5 that we are free in Christ from the burden and yoke of slavery of the Law.

The prayer for the readers of this book is that through the *Fellowship* of the Holy Spirit, they will have a freedom and openness of mind. The prayer is that they will have a refinement of understanding about the topic of baptism and grasp the expanse of what it means to be baptized by God's grace.

There are many questions that linger because of the focus church institutions and denominations have put on baptism. Is a ritual of water necessary? What is the proper method of this water event? Is it sprinkling an infant or submersion after a confession of faith? Is there really a command to partake of a water event? When is the right time or age to experience this water activity? Does this physical action provide salvation? Does the water have to be "living" or fresh-running? What does one baptism mean? Volumes of manuals have been written attempting to answer these questions. The results end up generating greater disagreements, arguments, and debates to the point of dividing the global church.

What has happened throughout history is that Christendom became focused on the method or mode of a physical water event, which has limited the definition of baptism and hindered the beautiful teaching of the Word of God of the larger concept of the *Baptism of Grace*. All the above questions are the wrong questions with the wrong focus. Here is the question we should be asking:

What does it mean to receive the baptism
of the Lord?

Confusion occurs when the definition of baptism is limited to a water event as people read and teach the Word of God. If this definition is applied to every biblical text with the word *baptism*, there is a danger of missing the point and the author's intent of the true meaning and concept of the text. The interpretation of biblical texts requires the reader to understand the whole biblical concept of what the author is communicating. Limiting the concept to just a water event can skew a person's understanding and lose the vast meaning of what Scripture intended.

Hebrews 5:11–6:20 warns us to move past the elementary instructions of repentance from dead works and faith in God, teaching about baptism, laying on of hands, the resurrection of the dead, and eternal judgment. As mature disciples, we must move past these basic concepts and probe more deeply into understanding heavenly thoughts, God's promises, and the actions of a true follower of Christ. The call is to move beyond the milk of the earthly, physical water baptism event and delve into a broader comprehension of the principles of baptism.

A full perception of the various baptisms is necessary to grasp the depth of God's instructions in His Word. Baptism is used in the Bible in multiple forms. Sometimes it is used as an illustration, sometime as an action, and other times as a mindset or condition of the heart. But the most important is the function of what the Lord does to or for us. Our challenge is to be diligent in identifying how the term *baptism* is used and what the author's original intent conveyed. When this approach is strictly adhered to, we discover five different baptisms throughout the Bible. The culmination of these five baptisms is the *Baptism of Grace*.

First, an investigation is required on how the word *baptism* is defined, how it was historically used, and the impact of the current modern definition.

Defining Baptism

History has abundantly proved that water baptism in its various forms has had the same harsh effect as the law; often working wrath and bringing believers in servitude to rules and forms, all in opposition to the liberty in Christ and to the freedom of God's wondrous grace in Christ, while it often divides the true believers.[1]

—Harry Bultema

Volumes of books and articles have been written by many professors, pastors, and priests whose works span hundreds of years, all with the attempt to obtain the proper definition, mode, and action of baptism. Reading many books and articles written by the church fathers to current-day authors leaves us frustrated, confused, and discouraged because the majority are written to

---

1. Harry Bultema, *The Bible and Baptism: A Re-Examination* (Muskegon, MI: Bultema Memorial Publication Society, 1955), 16.

support a single, narrow vision of baptism and attack someone else's physical water event practices. They are a sad commentary on these tremendous pieces of work and exhaustive efforts many people put into documenting their beliefs and positions. What becomes very apparent is that authors quote the same biblical passages to support their positions, and yet their conclusions for what the text means are diverse.

Here is the question all these books and articles generate about baptism:

If the Bible is clear that there is one baptism, then why are there such vast differences of opinion in definition, mode, and method?

Challenging thought:

The definition of baptism has been molded into a human-made activity focused on a narrow understanding of an earthly, physical water event, which ignores the vast and beautiful biblical concept of God's Baptism of Grace.

What has evolved is a cultural, human-focused religious ritual of an earthly, physical water event called baptism. It requires church attendees to line up with an institution's beliefs and doctrines. Constitutions, bylaws, creeds, and regulations have been written explaining what a Christian is to believe and the physical acts they are to perform to become a member of an institution. Splits have occurred, new denominations were created, more laws were written, and strict doctrines were developed as a result. While all of this was happening, the significance of the ritual method varied from a requirement of bodily submerging in flowing water to basins of water, to sprinkling infants, to a backyard dunk in a swimming pool, to even an act in a house bathtub. It has even permeated into requiring people to be dunked underwater in a dirty, dysentery-infected river. Beyond the uncertainty of this physical act is a more critical debate about the necessity of this act in order to obtain salvation.

Here is the repeated question:

Where is unity and one baptism?

Jesus dealt with this same issue in Matthew 21:23–27. The chief priests and elders (religious officials) came to Him and asked Him what authority He had to clear out the temple, heal the blind and lame, and condemn trees for not producing fruit. Jesus, in His classic way, issued them a challenge that if they could answer His question, He would answer theirs. Matthew 21:25 is a timeless question: "The baptism of John was from what source, from heaven or from men?" The depth of this question perplexed the great spiritual minds of the day. They realized that regardless of what answer they gave, they would look bad. If they answered from heaven, Jesus would tell them to change and believe Him. If they answered from John, that would dethrone them from their self-elevated positions. So they answered, "We do not know." What a tragedy! Their ambivalence and lack of humility to learn hindered them from understanding the Lord's authority and becoming true disciples.

Is there any difference today?

The question remains the same: Does baptism come from heaven or from people?

The focus has been narrowed to a human, physical water activity, and massive organizations have revolved around that activity. Christendom has become trapped just like the religious officials Jesus addressed. If today's answer is that baptism is from heaven, then why is the church so adamant about a specific method and process when we know the Lord works in each individual uniquely? If the answer is that it is from people, then the church must admit that the physical event is meaningless.

Ironically, in all the volumes I studied in my research for this book, the passage of Jesus's dialogue with the religious officials in Matthew 21:25 was never referenced or addressed. To broaden the scope of the topic of baptism, the same question Jesus asked of the first-century religious officials needs to be answered today:

Baptism—is it from heaven or from humans?

What Does Baptism Mean?

Exhaustive time and energy have been put into discovering a definition of baptism. Every writing wrestles with the research to develop the perfect description of the words *baptize* and *baptism*. Reconstructing the etymology of baptism has become the key to interpreting its meaning and how it is used in liturgical documentation. Defining baptize and baptism by grasping the concepts of the terms conveyed in the original language has resulted in many interpretations of these words. Theologians, pastors, and professors have poured a lifetime of hard work into the topic of baptism, and each one is to be admired for their servant-minded dedication in searching history, culture, and the Scriptures in the quest to clarify the mystery of baptism.

In the appendix at the back of this book are research notes and references that show the work of many authors who strove to obtain a good definition of baptism. The appendix provides a quick glimpse of the multiple and various conclusions regarding the definition of baptize and baptism. To summarize these tremendous works, the following list shows the magnitude of the variations that have been derived for the definition of the concept of baptism.

- immersion
- submersion
- emergence
- to pour over
- to sprinkle water over
- ceremony
- symbol
- washing
- purification
- intusposition
- to steep
- to merse
- to whelm
- to purify
- to intoxicate
- to dip
- sacrament
- rite of initiation
- to drown
- affected by controlling influence
- overwhelm by pouring
- submerging so as to never emerge
- to suffocate within a fluid

God's people today are greatly indebted to those who invested the energy in such great research to develop solid positions and justifications for what they believed to be the definition(s) of baptism. Many other exhaustive works on this controversial topic have not been cited, but the positions and points are similar, and adding them would only be redundant. As evidenced by the above list, a vast spectrum of definitions of baptism has been formed. This range of the definitions alone has caused irresolvable conflicts and created divisions between God's people.

Here are two questions the above list does not answer:

Which definition is correct?

What is the correct mode of baptism?

The above list predominantly centers on a physical water activity, which limits the full biblical understanding of the *Baptism of Grace*. A water event as part of the definition has become our cultural understanding of the term *baptism*. This limitation has resulted in a restricted understanding of God's truth and the conceptual depths of the apostles' writings. Baptism in the Bible has a much broader conceptual meaning and multiple varying definitions, depending on the context and the author's intended message.

My proposal to answer the two questions is that all the definitions are correct. One is not better than the other, nor should they be mutually exclusive. God works uniquely with each individual. He challenges each person according to where they are in their walk with Him. He corrects everyone according to their individual conduct. Everyone's process toward choosing to follow Christ is different. So it is only consistent that in God's economy, baptism is variable and individual. The intention of this postulation is not to condemn or discredit anyone who has participated in any type of specific baptismal activity, but rather to encourage whatever action was taken to be only the first step toward understanding the deeper mysteries of God.

The vast definitions of baptism denote the concept of an object completely smothered, inundated, saturated, and enveloped into some other entity. To help understand this concept, the illustrations most often used are the dyeing of a garment by immersing the object in colored water. Another illustration is drawing out water by dipping a vessel in and filling it up. The key point is that the word *baptism* is the process of completely submerging an object into something else. A literal, modern illustration is the deep-frying of a Thanksgiving turkey by baptizing it in hot oil. Science uses a term called *supersaturation*, which is when one component is excessively added to a second component, and the second component cannot absorb the totality of the first component. This is a beautiful picture of what God does to us by overflowing us with His loyal love, forgiveness, and grace. This is the concept we need to grasp as we study through the baptisms found in the Bible.

Instead of answering the specific questions regarding the *what* and *how* of baptism, we will study and seek a broader perspective of how God baptizes His people. Next, we need to understand a little history of how baptism evolved in the Christian church.

History

To understand the evolution of religious positions regarding the method, mode, and necessity of baptism, a review of history is crucial. Starting in the Old Testament, we find numerous types of washings that God required.

In Exodus 40:12–15 and Numbers 8:6–8, God told Moses that Aaron and his sons were to be washed by sprinkling purified water on them. God required a bronze laver placed in the tabernacle between the tent of meeting and the altar to be used for Aaron and his sons to wash their hands and feet before they approached the altar (Exod. 30:17–21). Leviticus 8:5–6 documents Moses washing Aaron and his sons during their ordination into the initial priesthood. This ordination included Aaron putting on special garments, the pouring of oil, and animal sacrifices for blood that was used as prophetic illustrations. Blood was applied to Aaron's ear lobe, the thumb of his right hand, and the big toe of his right foot. Aaron and his sons were the priests of the nation of Israel whose responsibility was to perform the sacrifices and offerings to the Lord that absolved the sins of the people. What a great precursor to Christ, who was ordained through John's water baptism, washed with oil from Mary, dressed with a royal robe by the Romans, and bled from the head (crown of thorns), hands, and feet on the cross. The washings were for the High Priest and priests, not for the general public. When Jesus finished His work on the cross, He eliminated the need for continual washings. His cross exploit was the final High Priest task, and it is never to be performed again.

In Numbers 19, God instituted a process for purification of sin that consisted of the ashes of a red heifer mixed in a vessel full of water from a flowing source. This mixture was used to remove impurities when someone touched a corpse. Contact with any-thing dead made a person unclean, which required purification. The priest cleansed them by sprinkling the purified water and heifer ash mixture onto the person or objects that had touched the dead person. This is a precursor of Jesus being the living water who removes our impurities and conquered the penalty of death.

The only time the multitudes of people were ever sprinkled by a liquid is found in Exodus 24:7–8 when Moses finished reading the book of the covenant. Moses sprinkled the sacrificial blood on the people and declared this blood the blood of the covenant of the Lord. This is another great foreshadowing of what Jesus did when He shed His blood on the cross as the final sacrifice, ushering in the New Covenant we are under today as prophesied in Ezekiel 36:22–38.

Hebrews 9:10 explains that the functions and action for cleansing were only "food and drink and various washings," external cleaning necessary until the time of the new order. The outward ceremony of washing was not sufficient; something better was required. Hebrews continues by indicating that the Law required bloodshed before forgiveness was provided (Heb. 9:22). It explains that Christ initiated a change. The work of Christ on the cross took away the first order of rituals and replaced it with the second order—faith and freedom from the Law and its physical requirements, "once for all" (Heb. 10:9–10).

The great transition from a physical religion to the spiritual relationship is beautifully conveyed in Hebrews 10:19–22. Because of the blood of Jesus, we now live by a new and living way. Because of the blood of Jesus, our hearts are cleansed, and our bodies are washed with pure and living water, which is Christ Himself. The book of Hebrews tells us that the blood of Jesus is our pure mechanism for forgiveness. It confirms that Jesus is the High Priest, and because of His work on the cross as the perfect, comprehensive sacrifice that covers all sin, we have direct access to the "throne of grace" (Heb. 4:16).

The work is done, and we do not need to perform any additional physical actions.

The nation of Israel was God's instrument of proclaiming His glory to the world. When a proselyte converted to Judaism, they were required to go through a ceremonial washing, and the males were circumcised.[1] At the time of John the Baptizer's arrival, the priesthood had become corrupt by power, politics, and money. John was in line to become a priest through the heritage of his father, Zechariah. John, however, separated himself from the religious corruption and started preaching the true message of Israel and its God—repentance. The method of forgiveness through the temple sacrifices was corrupt and meaningless in God's sight. David, in his pleading prayer to God for repentance

1. Edmund P. Clowney, *The Church* (Downers Grove, IL: InterVarsity Press, 1995), 276–277.

in Psalm 51:17, said, "A broken and a contrite heart, O God, You will not despise." John understood this and preached the truth of forgiveness, which is repentance that comes from the heart and a humble attitude. Because of his separation from the temple and still being under the Law, the only mechanism John had for symbolizing the cleansing was the ceremonial washing in the water of the Jordan River.

Quintus Septimius Florens Tertullianus wrote a homily on baptism in the second century that responds to a woman he called a female viper from the Cainite sect because of her proclamation that baptism is not necessary. Tertullianus's homily expresses that the necessity of baptism relates back to creation when water was a key element God used. He also relates the flood as the earth being baptized. He takes the position that the waters of baptism are sacred with cleansing and saving abilities administered to it by the Holy Spirit.

Tertullianus said this about baptism:

> We have indeed a second washing, it too a single one, that of blood, of which our Lord said, I have a baptism to be baptized with, when he had already been baptized. For he had come by water and blood, as John has written, so as to be baptized with water and glorified with blood. Likewise, so as to give us our vocation by water and our election by blood, he sent forth these two baptisms from out of the wound of his pierced side, because those who had faith in his blood were to be washed in water, and those who had washed in water would need also to be washed in blood.[2]

2. Tertullian, "Homily on Baptism," 35–41, http://www.tertullian.org/articles/evans_bapt/evans_bapt_index.htm.

In this homily, Tertullianus also dictated rules regarding the process of the water act but never addressed the blood washing:

> *The supreme right of giving it belongs to the high priest, which is the bishop: after him, to the presbyters and deacons, yet not without commission from the bishop, on account of the Church's dignity. . . . Those who are at the point of entering upon baptism ought to pray, with frequent prayers, fastings, bendings of the knee, and all-night vigils, along with the confession of all their former sins.*[3]

Here is where we must raise some red flags. Tertullianus is correct in stating that the supreme right to baptize is the High Priest's. However, this is not the bishop; it is Jesus Christ the High Priest as defined in Hebrews 8:1 and 9:11–12. Jesus the High Priest baptizes us. What the church has done over the years is develop human-made expectations, rules, methods, processes, and provisions that are completely irrelevant.

Who is this woman Tertullianus references who challenged the church? If it were not a woman, would they have listened? Was she right? Was she talking about the water event initiated by humans? Did she have a deeper understanding that the real baptism comes from the Lord and not by a human-made act? Because of Tertullianus's homily, it appears that his position as bishop was threatened. His intentions may have been pure, and his desire may have been to disciple the people he was teaching. What transpired may not have been his intention, but this teaching impacted the approach toward baptism throughout church history.

---

3. Tertullian, "Homily on Baptism," 35–41, http://www.tertullian.org/articles/evans_bapt/evans_bapt_index.htm.

Over the course of the years, the church's position on the function of baptism has continually been a source of controversy and evolution. Baptism (focusing on water) was important to the early church. The church believed that water was part of the saving process. As the church became more Gentile, the institution of catechism (a three-year instruction on Christian beliefs) evolved and was required before a person could become baptized in water. The early church met the first day of the week for a communion service where only those who were baptized in water could attend. The early church baptism was an act ideally performed by immersion in living, fresh-running water. In cases where water was scarce or a person was in poor health, the administration of baptism was performed by pouring water over their head three times.[4]

It is not clear if the early church baptized infants. But by 1215, it was clear that the church embraced infant baptism as a result of the creed documented by the Fourth Lateran Council, which states in part:

> The sacrament of baptism is celebrated in water by prayer to God and each person of the Trinity separately, that is to say, the Father, the Son, and the Holy Spirit. Duly conferred on both infants and adults by any one at all in the form appointed by the church, it promotes our salvation.[5]

---

4. Justo L. González, *The Story of Christianity: The Early Church to the Dawn of the Reformation* (New York: HarperCollins Publishers, 1984), 70, 96–97, 128.
5. John H. Leith, ed., *Creeds of the Churches* (Louisville, KY: John Knox Press, 1982), 58.

In 1517, Martin Luther, the primary proponent of the Reformation, concluded that there were these two sacraments instituted by Christ and physical signs of the promise of the gospel: communion and baptism. Today's church still holds these two sacraments as critical in the life and salvation of the people. Luther believed that baptism and faith were closely tied but did not believe that one must have faith before being baptized. His argument for infant baptism evolved around the theology that a person develops a believing faith through the gift of God and not by human work.[6] Luther believed that salvation was the work of God and baptism was a human action that only symbolizes a person's alignment with the gospel of Christ.

The Reformation generated an uprising of a school of thought labeled Anabaptist. Their position was that a person had to make a public confession of faith before a "real baptism" was performed. Since the time of Constantine (AD 306–337) until the Reformation, there was a strong alliance between the Catholic Church and government. When the Anabaptists proclaimed that infant baptism was not valid, they became outcasts from the church. Not only did they become an enemy of the church for heresy, but they also became seditionists against the government.

In 1528, Charles V ordered the Anabaptists to be put to death based on an ancient Roman law where everyone guilty of rebaptizing was to be put to death. Many were killed by drowning, burning, torturing, or being drawn and quartered, all because of their belief in how and when to perform an earthly physical water event.[7] It is horrific that Christians persecuted

---

6. Justo L. González, *The Story of Christianity: The Reformation to the Present Day* (New York: HarperCollins Publishers, 1985), 33–35.
7. Ibid., 53–56.

and murdered Christians because of a belief in an earthly, physical water event action.

Today, many Christian religious denominations follow the same pattern. They may not actually instill physical harm on people, but they do make it clear that people must perform the water event in accordance with their human-developed doctrine. When pastors, elders, or staff members are challenged to defend their position regarding the act of immersing a person in water, they can become very angry and struggle with articulating the necessity in their own words and supported by the whole Word of God.

Church institution attendance and membership have been denied because people do not feel led by the Lord to get rebaptized by immersion. Their parents in full faith had them baptized as an infant, and out of honor and respect, they choose not to comply. Many times within the church institution today, people are denied and eliminated from fellowshipping because of a human-developed, doctrinal, earthly, physical water event. How different is today's staunch position of the church institution regarding an earthly, physical water event to the position of the church in the 1500s? Many people today are hurt, lost, lonely, and outcast because of the church institution's dogmatic positions on an earthly, physical water event. It has torn Christendom apart for centuries.

This is far from an exhaustive historical study of baptism. The intent of including this discussion is to show that the church institution's belief and definition of baptism have migrated and become dangerous throughout history. Doctrinal positions on baptism have created significant damage to Christendom over the years. The biblical church fellowship, as taught in 1 John, is predicated on believing and having faith that Jesus Christ is the Messiah, the Son of God. This belief is the core component that bodies of believers should use as the litmus test of accepting someone into fellowship. John never writes that a physical water act is required as acceptance into fellowship with the children of God.

There is concern today about why people are not attending church and why so many churches are closing their doors. On the flip side, many are flocking to churches where they can be anonymous and blend into the crowd. They do not want to deal with dogmatic doctrine or go through some initiation ritual to become a church institution member. Maybe one reason is the ongoing controversy around baptism and the fact that intelligent, logical people understand that salvation is received by God's free grace obtained through faith. Yet the church institution requires them to participate in a physical event.

The humanity-to-God relationship has transitioned from the physical, as documented in the Old Testament, to the spiritual, as seen in the New Testament. Bultema uses the phrase "do religion to done religion."[8] Jesus came to fulfill the Law, and He emphasizes during His presentation on the mount (Matt. 5–7) that the righteousness structure is not physical actions but our heart and mind motives. He died as the "once for all" sacrifice (Heb. 9). He was the fulfillment of the New Covenant (Heb. 8). The New Covenant provides an individual relationship with God, instilling His Spirit in everyone (Jer. 31; John 14–16).

In the New Covenant (the age we live in today) there is not a need for any religious physical activity for salvation or being a member of an assembly of God's people. Jesus eliminated the requirements for sacrifices, which rendered the temple and the

---

8. Harry Bultema, *The Bible and Baptism: A Re-Examination* (Muskegon, MI: Bultema Memorial Publication Society, 1955), 42.

altars useless. Therefore, God allowed the temple to be destroyed in AD 70. Acts 2 documents believers receiving the promised Holy Spirit, finalizing the transition from God relating to humanity in physical, corporate form to God relating spiritually and individually with people.

New Covenant believers have an individualized, spiritual relationship with the Lord, so when it comes to baptism, we must evaluate the depth of what the New Testament teaches. Mainstream Christendom today has a myopic focus solely on the earthly, physical water event. The next chapters challenge believers to study and evaluate the wonderful magnitude of the *Baptism of Grace* that the Lord instills in them. There is also a challenge that church institutions expand their thinking and comprehend the fullness of the five baptisms found in the New Testament.

Baptisms in the Bible

When we come across *baptize* or *baptism* while reading and studying God's Word, here are the questions we should ask: What baptism? What is the message of the text? Is the term referring to an action, a concept, or a result? There are five baptisms in Scripture: water, Trinity, Holy Spirit, fire, and blood. All these baptisms have different facets and characteristics, so as we come across the term *baptism* in the text, we must decipher how it applies to what the author is trying to convey.

As believers and followers of Christ, we must understand and grasp the meaning of how each baptism is used. As the understanding of the five baptisms becomes clearer, a deeper knowledge of God's grace evolves. God's Word becomes more meaningful and relevant when an expanded meaning of baptism is used in the appropriate context. Understanding the biblical significance and meaning of all five baptisms is critical if we are to fully understand how to live the Christian life and follow the Lord. The first baptism we will explore is water baptism.

Water Baptism

> *John the Baptist appeared in the wilderness preaching*
> *a baptism of repentance for the forgiveness of sins. And*
> *all the country of Judea was going out to him, and all*
> *the people of Jerusalem; and they were being baptized*
> *by him in the Jordan River, confessing their sins.*
>
> —Mark 1:4–5

In the Gospels, John is introduced as the Baptizer. John's baptism was an earthly, physical activity centered on water that symbolized the ceremonial washings (discussed earlier). His message was for people to have a heart of repentance. The baptism John performed was during the temple animal sacrificial era. That era went back to the Passover in Exodus, and the means for expressing repentance was through the ritual ceremonial events of shedding animal blood and burning it on the altar as a pleasant aroma to God (Exod. 29:18). When John came on the scene, the priests and religious government were full of corruption, greed, and legalism that lost focus on the real heart condition God wants—justice, loving kindness, and walking humbly with Him (Micah 6:6–8).

The repentance activity John conducted was a completely different ritual than any previous religious ordinance for confessing sin. John's motive was to refocus the people from the oppressive and restrictive religious legalism the Pharisees were requiring. He wanted to get people to understand that admission of sin, a godly heart, and righteous living are what God truly desires (Ps. 51). That only comes when a person has a contrite heart and chooses to follow the Lord's commands and guidance. The evidence of a person's following of Christ is their daily lifestyle, not just performing a religious, physical ritual (Eph. 2:8–9).

One intriguing, recorded water baptism is documented in Acts 8:34–40. Philip shared the gospel of Jesus and baptized the eunuch in water. Like any story or passage in the Bible, this event requires an in-depth study of the context without excluding any part of the recorded event. The strangest element of this event is that after the earthly, physical water activity, Philip was snatched up by the Spirit of the Lord. Instead of just reading through this event and moving on, ask this question: Why did that happen? A possible answer might be that the Lord did not want the eunuch to think Philip had anything to do with his salvation and that the Spirit is the protagonist of the story. This display of power is the main point of Luke documenting an event that moved the focus from any earthly, physical activity to the power and reality of the Holy Spirit. It was not what Philip did. It was not about the physical water act. The story (consistent throughout the Word of God) is about the Lord. It is about the Holy Spirit, the third person of the Trinity. It is about the Holy Spirit's role in salvation.

John the Baptizer's mission transitioned from a message of repentance through a physical action to "Behold, the Lamb of God who takes away the sin of the world" (John 1:29). John's mission was transformed from a focus on the physical water to Christ the living water. Philip's mission transformed from performing an earthly physical act to the Holy Spirit taking him completely out of the scene so the eunuch's focus would be only on the Lord. Eusebius of Caesarea in his writings about John the Baptizer captures this transition from the physical to the spiritual:

> *I think the desert here is a symbol of that which of old was void of all God's good things, I mean the Church of the Gentiles, and the river by the desert that cleanses all that are bathed therein is a figure of some cleansing*

spiritual power, of which the Scriptures speak, saying, "The movements of the river make glad the city of God." And this means the ever-flowing stream of the Holy Spirit welling from above and watering the city of God, which is the name for life according to God. This river of God, then, has reached even unto the desert, that is the Gentile Church, and even now supplies it with the living water that it bears.[1]

The Apostle John in all three of his documentations discusses another type of water baptism, one that is completely different from the physical washing that John the Baptizer performed. As recorded in the Gospel of John, Jesus says, "Truly, truly, I say to you, unless one is born of water and Spirit he cannot enter into the kingdom of God" (John 3:5). Jesus is discussing with Nicodemus the concept of being born again. He is illustrating to Nicodemus that to enter the kingdom of heaven, a change must occur that is outside human capabilities.

Nicodemus and John would not have a clear understanding of the Holy Spirit like we do today. Jesus referenced a heavenly intervention of the water and the Spirit provided from the Lord Almighty that is written about in Isaiah 44:3–5. He was also referring to Ezekiel 37:9–10 when the breath and wind from heaven caused the bones in the valley to turn into a great army. Jesus teaches that this water and Spirit (Spirit, spirit, or wind, depending on the translation) comes from the Lord God above who does the work of regeneration. Jesus then tells Nicodemus

---

1. *Eusebius of Caesarea: Demonstratio Evangelica.* Trans. W. J. Ferrar (1920), Book 9, Chapter 6, http://www.tertullian.org/fathers/eusebius_de_11_book9.htm.

that the way to eternal life is to believe in the only begotten Son of God (John 3:15–16).

The message for us is to listen to the prompting of the Holy Spirit and believe in the Son of God. It is then that the Father regenerates us and gives us an inheritance in His kingdom (Rom. 8).

John documents the event of Jesus's encounter with a Samaritan woman at a physical water well (John 4:4–26, 39–42). Jesus tells the woman, "If you knew the gift of God, and who it is who says to you, 'Give Me a drink,' you would have asked Him, and He would have given you living water" (John 4:10). Then Jesus tells her, "Everyone who drinks of this water will thirst again; but whoever drinks of the water that I will give him shall never thirst; but the water that I will give him will become in him a well of water springing up to eternal life" (John 4:13–14). Jesus offers this woman "living water," which is Himself. What is interesting is what Jesus did not do. If an earthly, physical event were critical, necessary, or required, Jesus would have performed that ritual right there with this woman. Instead, He gives the woman His living water, which is sin-cleansing and eternal life. The result of this encounter was that the woman became an evangelist for the Messiah. She received the living water of Jesus and then, as a result, proclaimed who He was and what He had done for her.

In a commanding profession to the temple crowd, Jesus stands up and shouts, "If anyone is thirsty, let him come to Me and drink. He who believes in Me, as the Scripture said, 'From his innermost being will flow rivers of living water'" (John 7:37–38). In the next verse, John explains that Jesus was referring to the Holy Spirit as the continual outflow of the living water. At the end of John's vision in Revelation, the water of life that generates from Christ and the throne of God (Rev. 22:1) is the essential element of eternal life and salvation. In Revelation 21:6, Jesus says, "It is done. I am the Alpha and the Omega, the beginning and the end. I will give to the one who thirsts from the spring of the water of life without cost." Revelation 22:16–17 states that the outflow of salvation is the Holy Spirit and the church of Christ.

Jesus is the living water that flows out from the Father. Jesus baptizes (fills, covers, immerses, supersaturates) us with His living water of salvation and eternal life. Then Jesus, through the living water, sends the Holy Spirit who becomes the influencer in the life of those who believe. The evidence of the Holy Spirit in the believer's life is the down payment and seal of eternal life that the living water (Jesus) provides (Eph. 1:13–14). The continual flow of the truths of Christ, the gospel of salvation, and promised eternal life emanates through the living water in which Jesus submerges us.

The evidence of the baptism of the living water is recognized by how the Holy Spirit infiltrates our actions. Through individuals, the gifts and fruit of the Holy Spirit flow into Christ's assembly of people. Acts 1:8 says that believers *will* be witnesses when the Holy Spirit comes upon them. Those who believe that Jesus is the Son of God are baptized by Jesus with living water that saturates them with the Holy Spirit. The result is a living river of sharing the truth, witnessing, and teaching that never stops, just like the woman at the well.

Water baptism is more comprehensive than just an earthly, physical immersion or sprinkling action. It is being submerged and influenced by the saving work of Jesus Christ. It is knowing that we are covered by the grace of God through the sacrifice of Jesus. It is confidence that we have eternal life and an inheritance because of the presence of the Holy Spirit whom Jesus sent through the living water.

The living water baptism is performed by the Lord! He does the work when we believe that Jesus is the Son of God. We become baptized (immersed, influenced, saturated) with the outflow of the living water administered by the Lord alone. When this happens, true believers will witness and teach about the Lord. The evidence of a true believer baptized by the living water is someone who must share and communicate the saving grace of the Lord. The church that consists of believers who have the outflowing of the living water is a church that is alive. Alive churches proclaim the Word of God that flows out to the community and the world. That is the living water baptism that is consistent with the entire biblical message. The Lord's people have the responsibility to show the world the living, almighty God.

Water baptism is being submerged, influenced, and saturated by the living water (Jesus Christ and the Holy Spirit) that gives us eternal life, making us the Lord's witness forever.

Trinity Baptism

Go therefore and make disciples of all the nations, baptizing them in the name of the Father and the Son and the Holy Spirit, teaching them to observe all that I commanded you; and lo, I am with you always, even to the end of the age.

—Matt. 28:19–20

Context is very important when we study any Scripture. To correctly understand what the original author is communicating, we must grasp the overall message of the whole writing. All interpretations of any part of the Word of God must ensure purity to the immediate text, the specific author's intent, and the whole of the Bible. The above verses from Matthew 28 are at the conclusion of Matthew's writing to the Jews, confirming that Jesus is the Messiah King. The whole thesis of Matthew is that Jesus is the Messiah, the promised Son of God, and the One the prophets foretold. To the Jews, the Trinity (Father, Son, and Holy Spirit) was a foreign concept. For centuries, their worship was to one God (Yahweh). When Jesus was on earth, many Jews would not believe He was the Son of God or that He was God. This concept was blasphemy, and because Jesus claimed to be God, they had Him killed. In the context and theme of Matthew, the concluding message from Jesus to the disciples is for them to teach about the three-in-one God—the Father, the Son, and the Holy Spirit.

Jesus issues a directive to His disciples. These verses have been labeled the Great Commission. But what is the command that Jesus really gave the disciples? There are three actions the disciples were to perform.

1. Make disciples.
2. Baptize people in (into) the Father, Son, and Holy Spirit.
3. Teach people to obey His commandments.

The second action is a stumbling block to Christendom. Because of the narrow view of baptism (*baptizo*), the translation of this statement is used to support an earthly, physical water event. By expanding the thought process of baptism to something far greater than a physical act, this directive becomes more meaningful. The context of these verses is not associated with water. Instead of limiting the definition of the word *baptism* to a physical water event, insert the words and concepts listed earlier. If the preconception that water is involved in this text is eliminated and we insert conceptual words such as *influence, intoxicate, suffocate,* and *overwhelm,* the complexity of the directive Jesus gave to His disciple is much broader.

The translation of the phrase "baptizing them in" is critical for understanding this directive from the Lord. In Greek, the phrase is βαπτίζοντες αὐτοὺς εἰς. How the word εἰς (eyes) is translated impacts the meaning and understanding of the intent of this command. When translating εἰς there are several possible meanings, including into, unto, to, toward, for, and among.[2]

To further assess the translative impact on our understanding of the full Bible contextual view of the baptism concept, look at Romans 6:3: "Or do you not know that all of us who have been baptized *into* Christ Jesus have been baptized *into* his death?" (emphasis added). Let's look at the Greek ἐβαπτίσθημεν εἰς Χριστὸν [Ἰησοῦν].[3] Galatians 3:27 is translated, "For all of you who were baptized *into* Christ." The same Greek word is translated differently in Matthew 28. The topic is the same, and the concept is the same, so why is "into" used in Romans and Galatians and not in Matthew? It should be the same. Matthew 28:19 should read, "baptizing them *into* the name of the Father and the Son and the Holy Spirit" (emphasis added). That provides consistency through the Word of God and changes the focus from an earthly, physical water act to immersion into the Triune God.

If we translate the Greek word "to influence" or "become under the influence of" and understand that the concept is about an object fully submerged *into* something, the perspective of this directive changes. A person submerged *into* water comes out wet. Every part of the body is influenced by the water. If it is cold water,

---

2. "Baptizing them in," *Strong's Concordance*, Matthew 28:18–19, 1519, https://lumina.bible.org/bible/Matthew+28.
3. Ibid.

the body temperature will be influenced by the water temperature. A white shirt submerged *into* red dye will come out red. The shirt color was influenced by the red dye. Hot steel submerged *into* cold water is a process of hardening the steel. The cold water influenced the steel by changing its molecular structure and causing strong, hardened steel. A mind that reads and watches (is submerged in) violence is influenced by violence when dealing with issues. A mind that is submerged *into* the Word of God will be influenced to act in love when issues arise. Submerging an object *into* something that influences and impacts that object is the concept of the definition of baptism. Being baptized *into* the Father, Son, and Holy Spirit means to be influenced, changed, and impacted by the Triune God. This is the same concept that Jesus was teaching Nicodemus in John 3 regarding being born again.

Modern translations of Matthew 28:19–20 read like the verses at the beginning of this chapter. What may surprise many Christians today is that the phrase *baptizing them in the name of the Father and the Son and the Holy Spirit* may not have existed in the original text. This is an impediment for many denominations' doctrines that have been developed on this one phrase. The question regarding the originality of this phrase generates from studying Eusebius of Caesarea's writing before and after the Nicene Creed developed in AD 325. Today, the two earliest original texts (before the fourth century) of Matthew that are available are missing the last page, which includes the verses in question.

J. R. Ensey writes this in his article "The Great Commission in Luke":

> *To many scholars and textual analysts, the Matthean phrase obviously belongs to the post-apostolic age. It does not occur in any Greek manuscript before the*

fourth century, after the Nicene Council in A.D. 325. Before Nicea [sic], Eusebius consistently quotes it as ending with "in my name," but after Nicea [sic], the full phrase with the titles.[4]

According to William J. Morford, editor and translator of *The One New Man Bible*:

Matthew 28:19 in the Greek text contains a reference to Father, Son, and Holy Spirit. There is considerable evidence that this phrase was added at the Nicean [sic] Council in 325 AD. Several early Christian theologians, who had seen the complete book of Matthew, attested that the early copies of Matthew did not contain the phrase. Eusebius of Caesarea was one of those and even though he believed in the Trinity, he wrote that the phrase, "immersing in the name of the Father and of the Son and of the Holy Ghost" was not in the early texts. Today there are only two copies of Matthew earlier than the 4th C and the last page of the Codex of each of those was destroyed many centuries ago.[5]

F. C. Conybeare, professor of theology at the University of Oxford, discusses in his *History of New Testament Criticism* the challenge of the text in Matthew 28:19.

---

4. J. R. Ensey, "The Great Commission in Luke," *Advance Ministries*, November 2017, http://www.advanceministries.org/articles/articlepages/commission.htm.
5. William J. Morford, *One New Man Bible: Revealing Jewish Roots and Power* (Travelers Rest, SC: True Potential Publishing, 2011), 1750.

Here Eusebius, Bishop of Caesarea, who died about the year 340, and was entrusted by the Emperor Constantine with the task of preparing fifty éditions de luxe of the gospels for the great churches built or rebuilt after the Diocletian persecution was ended, read in such of his works as he wrote before the year 325 as follows, "Go ye therefore, and make disciples of all the nations in my name; teaching them," etc.

It is clear therefore, that of the MSS, which Eusebius inherited from his predecessor, Pamphilus, at Caesarea in Palestine, some at least preserved the original reading, in which there was no mention either of Baptism or of Father, Son, and Holy Ghost.[6]

W. J. Ferrar's translation of *Eusebius of Caesarea: Demonstratio Evangelica* shows that Eusebius did not include "baptizing in the name of the Father, Son, and Holy Spirit" in his early writings.[7]

If we accept the argument that the phrase *baptizing into the name of the Father, Son, and Holy Spirit* is not in the original text,

---

6. F. C. Conybeare, *History of New Testament Criticism* (New York: The Knickerbocker Press, 1910), 98–99.
7. *Eusebius: Son of Pamphilus: The Proof of the Gospel, Book I,* Trans. W. J. Ferrar, Chapter 6, http://www.tertullian.org/fathers/eusebius_de_03_book1.htm; *The Proof of the Gospel Being the Demonstratio Evangelica of Eusebius of Caesarea; Book III,* Chapter 6, 132 (a), 152 (Eusebius quotes Matthew 28:19: "With one word and voice He said to His disciples: 'Go, and make disciples of all nations in My Name, teaching them to observe all things whatsoever I have commanded you.'"); Chapter 7, 136 (a–d), 157 (Eusebius writes and quotes Matthew 28:19: "Go forth, and make disciples of all nations." "But how," the disciples might reasonably have answered. . . . But while the disciples of Jesus were most likely either saying thus, or thinking thus, the Master solved their difficulties, by the addition of one phrase, saying they should triumph "in MY NAME.").

then it brings into question the position of being baptized into the Trinity. The Nicene Creed, constructed in AD 325, was to address the heresy of Arius who promoted the theology that Jesus was a created being and not the Son of God. The creed was developed with the cooperation of 318 church fathers whose desire was to preserve and solidify that Jesus was the begotten Son of God and not created. The creed was written to confirm that there is one God consisting of the Father, Son, and Holy Spirit.[8] The belief is that from this point on, Matthew 28:19 included the phrase *baptizing into the name of the Father, Son, and Holy Spirit.*

If the phrase *baptizing into the name of the Father, Son, and Holy Spirit* was in the original text, then the argument for the Trinity baptism makes sense because up to this point, the Jews were immersed only in Yahweh the Father. Jesus then directs His disciples to teach the Trinitarian God: the Father, the Son the Messiah, and the Holy Spirit whom Jesus will send to dwell on the earth in His people. Guiding people toward Christian behavior, immersing them in the concept of the Trinity, and teaching them to love God and others is our "great commission."

If the phrase *baptizing into the name of the Father, Son, and Holy Spirit* was added after the Nicene Creed, then the argument for the Trinity baptism becomes the fact that 318 church fathers believed that it was necessary for future generations to understand the one God, three-person concept. To include it in the commission from Jesus documented in Matthew would validate the importance and protect against future heresies. The point of the Nicene Creed and the insertion of this phrase were to preserve, teach, and communicate the truth of the Trinity.

---

8. John H. Leith, ed., *Creeds of the Churches* (Louisville, KY: John Knox Press, 1982), 28–31.

Regardless of when the phrase became part of the Holy Scriptures we have today, the message is the same:

Be influenced by the one God consisting
of three persons.

Additional confirmation that our commission is to teach the Trinity influence is to evaluate how the apostles handled this concept. The writings of the apostles teach the Trinity without fail, defining the three-person Godhead! The apostles taught the Trinity consistently.

Paul incorporates in his epistles the theology of the interactions and roles of the Trinity (Rom. 1:1–5; 1 Cor. 1:30–2:13; 2 Cor. 1:18–22; Gal. 1:3–3:5; 4:6; Eph. 1:3–14; Phil. 1:12–20; Col. 1:1–8; 1 Thess. 1:1–5; 2 Thess. 2:13–14; 1 Tim. 3:14–4:1; 2 Tim. 1:8–14; Titus 3:3–7). The first three chapters of Hebrews is a detailed description of each person in the Trinity. James discusses the functions of the Trinity in James 4:5–12. Peter teaches the Trinity in 1 Peter 1:1–2, 16–21. John identifies the Trinity in 1 John 3:23–24. The crescendo of Paul's prayer for the saints in Ephesians 3:14–19 is that we would be strengthened with the power of the Holy Spirit, comprehend the vast love of Christ, and be filled with the fullness of the Father. The apostles understood the commission of teaching the Father, Son, and Holy Spirit, and ensured they included it in their writings that are preserved for us today. Every Bible class, sermon, lecture, song, and written document should include the three-person God in its message.

Being submerged into the full magnitude of God the Father, God the Son, and God the Holy Spirit results in understanding His grace, our inheritance, salvation, love, gifts, and the list goes on. The Triune God completely covers, encapsulates, and infiltrates us so we are wholly influenced by who and what He was, is, and will be.

Trinity baptism is a dynamic perpetual influencing force in our life that increases as we immerse into His Word and strive to comprehend the incomprehensible.

Holy Spirit Baptism

John testified saying, "I have seen the Spirit descending as a dove out of heaven, and He remained upon Him. I did not recognize Him, but He who sent me to baptize in water said to me, 'He upon whom you see the Spirit descending and remaining upon Him, this is the One who baptizes in the Holy Spirit.' I myself have seen, and have testified that this is the Son of God."

—John 1:32–34

All four Gospels record in detail the event of the Holy Spirit descending on Jesus. In addition, all four Gospels make it very clear that Jesus submerges (baptizes) humanity with the Holy Spirit (Matthew 3:11; Mark 1:8; Luke 3:16; John 1:33).

As quickly as Matthew introduces John the Baptizer[9] in chapter 3, he documents in verse 11 that Jesus will baptize with

---

9. Tradition calls John "John the Baptist." To eliminate confusion and separate his title from a major Christian denomination, "the Baptizer" is used. An even better title for John would be John the Proclaimer because that was his commission, to prepare the people for the Messiah (Luke 1:17) and announce the Messiah: "Behold, the Lamb of God who takes away the sin of the world!" (John 1:29).

the Spirit. John immersed in earthly, physical water, and Jesus immerses in the Spirit. Matthew then turns the focus on the event of John immersing Jesus in water, which resulted in an audible confession from the Father that Jesus is the Messiah and the presentation of the Holy Spirit. An important fact to focus on regarding Jesus's water baptism event is the introduction of the Holy Spirit to the world, a precursor to the New Covenant described in Jeremiah 31. Jesus was publicly baptized by John in the water, but more importantly, He was publicly baptized (submerged) by the Father with the Holy Spirit! Through this event, Jesus became influenced by the Holy Spirit. Right after this event, Matthew documents that the Holy Spirit led Jesus into the wilderness to fast for 40 days and be tempted by the devil.

Many attempts have been made to formulate how the Holy Spirit immersion works and when it happens. But just like salvation and spiritual growth, this is an individual experience and performed by Jesus. The immersion and influence of the Holy Spirit cannot be forced through a formulated ritual or demanding prayer; it is performed by Jesus how He desires, when He desires, and mostly in a unique personal manner.

So the question becomes, "How do I receive the Holy Spirit?" The answer is simple. We are called to believe in the Lord Jesus Christ, and He does the rest. His inundation of the Holy Spirit is a completely different and unique experience for everyone. This is a spiritual event that in most cases and for most people is unseen, subtle, and progressive.

A good parent would not give a loaded gun to a toddler and say to be careful. A good parent would not give a 600-horse-power, high-performance sports car to a 16-year-old who just got their license and say to have fun. Because of their love, a good parent who has the desire and ability to provide these gifts to their child would ensure the child has proper training, experience, capability, and proven responsibility before they are given something. Jesus does the same thing when providing the Holy Spirit, which is accompanied by power. "You will receive power when the Holy Spirit has come upon you" (Acts 1:8), "the surpassing greatness of His power toward us who believe" (Eph. 1:19). This is the same power that raised Christ from the dead. We must learn about this power, we must gain experience slowly regarding this power, we must show that we can handle this power, and we need to demonstrate we can handle the power responsibly.

Hebrews 6:1–5 calls us to maturity, warning us to leave the dead works of physical activities and pursue the heavenly gifts as partakers of the Holy Spirit. Jesus loves us so much that He keeps us from self-destructing by becoming prideful, self-promoting, or pursuing monetary gain because of this power. Jesus immerses each individual with the Holy Spirit depending on their circumstances and maturity. That is why Paul makes it clear in 1 Corinthians 12 that there are many spiritual gifts distributed to many individuals. There is no formula. Jesus does the Holy Spirit distribution in His timing and as necessary.

John baptizes in water; Jesus baptizes in the Holy Spirit. The influence of the Holy Spirit is what believers today should desire and seek. We live in the age of the church, which means we have an individualistic, spiritual relationship with the Lord. We need to stop chasing after physical rituals and seek the kingdom of heaven.

Ephesians 2:4–8 tells us that the same power of the Holy Spirit that raised Christ from the dead has raised us up and seated us with Jesus in the heavens. Grasp this: the Father provided a path of reconciliation through His Son, Jesus.

Because of the Son's sacrifice, the Holy Spirit raised Jesus from the dead and seated Him at the right hand of the Father. Jesus, in turn, provides the Holy Spirit for us, which raises us up to sit with the Triune God. This is a present condition. It means that today we are in the Lord's presence, communing with Him and living according to our inheritance as His child. That is the baptism we should desire.

The Holy Spirit baptism does not end with the Gospels. The book of Acts documents the transition process the disciples and apostles went through to discover how to live a spiritual life versus the previous physical, ritualistic, religious life. This spiritual life is what Paul refers to as living in the heavenly realms. Acts is very clear from the beginning of the book that a change took place and that an adjustment to the normalcy of religion made a dramatic shift. Those who followed Jesus were no longer required to perform sacrifices, present offerings, or observe feasts and festivals.

Those who believe that Jesus was the ultimate sacrifice once and forever no longer live under the requirement of performing earthly, physical functions for the forgiveness of sin and for salvation. Jesus is the mediator of the New Covenant (Heb. 9:14) that was prophesied in Jeremiah 31:31–34. God instills the knowledge of His requirements into every individual of every nationality, administered by the Holy Spirit (Joel 2:28–29).

What this means for us today is that there is not a standard or formula for being a Christian.

The book of Acts starts by documenting the physical appearance of the resurrected Messiah to many in Jerusalem.

66

Jesus commanded the disciples to stay in Jerusalem and wait for the promised Holy Spirit. Acts 1:4–5 documents this event where Jesus promises that He will baptize (influence) them (us) with the Holy Spirit. He contrasts this with the baptism (submersion) of water that John performed.

> *Gathering them together, He commanded them not to leave Jerusalem, but to wait for what the Father had promised, "Which," He said, "you heard of from Me; for John baptized with water, but you will be baptized with the Holy Spirit not many days from now."*
>
> —Acts 1:4–5

When God issues regulations throughout the Bible, they remain in effect until He changes them. An example is the requirement of animal sacrifices in the Pentateuch, regulations that were in place until the sacrifice of Jesus. Then, as documented in the book of Hebrews, Jesus changed the animal sacrifice requirement because He became the final sacrifice. The key word in the verses in Acts is *but*. That word alerts the reader that something different is coming. It ushers in an antithesis of the first statement. John baptized with water (old ritual), *but* you will be baptized with the Holy Spirit (New Covenant). In Acts 1:5, God changed the physical water baptism requirement to the Holy Spirit baptism requirement, fulfilling the New Covenant prophecy.

Here are the challenge questions. Which submersion do you want—John's or Jesus's? What form of influence do you want—earthly, physical water or the Holy Spirit? Which one saves you? The answer is Jesus's baptism with the Holy Spirit.

The following chart captures the work and influence the Holy Spirit has on our lives.

The Holy Spirit convicts us of our sin and our need for repentance and sanctifies us.	John 16:7–11; 1 Thessalonians 4:3–8; 2 Thessalonians 2:13–15; Hebrews 3:7–15; 1 Peter 1:1–2
We receive the gospel message of salvation from the Holy Spirit.	Matthew 10:17–20; Mark 13:9–11; Luke 12:11–12; John 14:26–27; 16:13–15; Romans 1:1–6; 1 Corinthians 2:10–16; 12:3–11; Ephesians 1:17; 3:2–6; 1 Thessalonians 1:4–10; Hebrews 10:15–18; 1 Peter 1:10–12; 2 Peter 1:19–21; 1 John 3:21–24; 4:13–15
The Holy Spirit gives us a clean, renewed life.	John 6:63; Romans 7:4–6; 1 Corinthians 6:9–11; Titus 3:3–8
There is a consistent call throughout the apostles' writings to be filled with and controlled by the Holy Spirit, which is the directive for Christians today.	Romans 8:1–17; 2 Corinthians 6:3–10; Galatians 5:16–18; Ephesians 2:19–22; 3:14–19; 5:15–20
Our seal and confidence that we are a child of God is the Holy Spirit.	John 14:15–17; Romans 5:1–5; 2 Corinthians 1:18–22; 5:5; Galatians 4:1–7; Ephesians 1:13–14; 2 Timothy 1:13–14
The Holy Spirit is our communication mechanism of prayer.	Romans 8:22–27; Jude 1:20–21
The gifts of the Holy Spirit distributed to humanity are God's testimony of Himself.	Romans 12:4–8; 1 Corinthians 12:4–11; 2 Corinthians 3:1–6; Galatians 5:22–26; Ephesians 4:11–12; Hebrews 2:1–4
We are to live a life pleasing to the Holy Spirit.	Matthew 12:30–32; Mark 3:28–29; Luke 12:8–10; John 7:37–39; Romans 15:13–16; 1 Corinthians 3:16–17; 6:18–20; Galatians 5:25; 6:7–10; Ephesians 4:29–5:1

Jesus supersaturates us with the Holy Spirit—an influence that convicts us of sin, teaches us the truth of Jesus Christ, gives us a new life, directs our conduct toward holiness, confirms our inheritance as children of God, provides a direct line of communication to the Father, and instills us with unique gifts. Mainstream Christendom teaches, challenges, and desires that everyone should experience these qualities. But these qualities are only achieved by Jesus overwhelming us with the Holy Spirit. They are qualities that can never be achieved through the sacrificial Law, human works, or an earthly, physical water event. Followers of Jesus the Messiah should bathe in His submersion of the Holy Spirit. We need to soak in the presence of the Spirit of God so the chart above becomes our character and DNA.

At the very beginning of Acts, Luke indicates that when the words *baptism* or *baptize* are used, they refer to Jesus's immersing, submerging, and influencing with the Holy Spirit. The event at Pentecost in Acts 2 is the fulfillment of the prophecy of Joel and the definition of Jesus baptizing with the Holy Spirit.

In Acts 8:14–17, Peter and John go to believers in Samaria and facilitate their immersion of the Holy Spirit. This text indicates that the people were only baptized by being immersed in earthly, physical water. The people of Samaria knew Jesus and believed, but the full immersion according to the New Covenant was not fulfilled because they had not received the Holy Spirit. Peter and John functioned as ambassadors of Jesus by facilitating the Holy Spirit descending (infiltrating, submerging) upon them.

Acts 9 covers Paul's encounter with Jesus on the road to Damascus. After this encounter, Ananias (at the Lord's prompting) visits Paul with a message.

So Ananias departed and entered the house, and after laying his hands on him said, "Brother Saul, the Lord Jesus, who appeared to you on the road by which you were coming, has sent me so that you may regain your sight and be filled with the Holy Spirit." And immediately there fell from his eyes something like scales, and he regained his sight, and he got up and was baptized; and he took food and was strengthened.

—Acts 9:17–19

In verse 17, we see that Ananias brought Paul two things: (1) renewed eyesight and (2) the filling of the Holy Spirit. So when we come to verse 18, the two things Paul received are (1) renewed eyesight and (2) baptism. In the context of verse 17, this is the baptism of the filling of the Holy Spirit.

Peter is one of the great characters in the Bible we can learn from through both his good and bad experiences. Peter walks on water yet loses focus on Jesus and starts sinking. Peter is willing to die for the Lord yet denies Him. After three years of seeing miracles and living under the teaching of the Messiah, Peter goes back to fishing after Christ's death. The final lesson from the Gospels comes when Jesus confirms Peter and tells him to make disciples, teach His people, and follow Him.

The account in Acts 10:1–11:18 is again another one of Peter's learning experiences. Cornelius, a centurion (Gentile), had a vision to invite Peter to come and share the gospel with him at the same time Peter had a vision where God illustrated the transition of the inclusion of the Gentiles into His family. At the end of chapter 10, Peter recognizes that while he is telling Cornelius about Jesus, the Holy Spirit was poured onto the Gentiles. Steeped in tradition, Peter then pursues earthly, physical water baptism for the Gentiles. To stop the study of this event at the end of chapter 10 is a tragedy because we would miss the lesson Peter learned. In Chapter 11, Peter testifies to the apostles and brethren in Jerusalem about the Gentile experience.

The event with Cornelius occurred in Caesarea, so at a minimum, Peter had the time it took to travel from Caesarea to Jerusalem to process what happened. At the end of Peter's presentation in Jerusalem, the lesson Peter learned was spelled out clearly. He remembered the words of Jesus: "John baptized with water, but you will be baptized with the Holy Spirit" (Acts 11:16). The light bulb came on, he got it, message received. It is about God giving the gift of the Holy Spirit. It is not about an earthly, physical ritual. The apostles and others also got it because their response was that God granted the Gentiles salvation and the gift of life through the Holy Spirit!

Right after this revelation that Luke documents in Acts 11, he continues by listing the characteristics of Barnabas who brought Saul (Paul) into a teaching position and built the church in Antioch. Barnabas's résumé consisted of a good man, full of faith, and full of the Holy Spirit. The transition in Acts pivots on the church at Antioch where the roots of the name *Christian* emanates. From this point, when Luke uses the term *baptism*, the definition we should consider is immersing into the Holy Spirit, the filling of the Holy Spirit, or the influencing of the Holy Spirit.

There are only three other uses of the word *baptism* after Acts 11. The type of baptism for Lydia (Acts 16:15) or the baptism of Paul and Silas's jailer (Acts 16:33) are not specifically identified. Understanding that the concept of baptism changed in the first chapter of Acts, from an earthly, physical water event to the influencing submerging of the Holy Spirit, we can make the deduction that Lydia and the jailer were baptized with the Holy Spirit. Knowing that the most meaningful baptism, as we learned from the apostles, was being influenced by the Holy Spirit, we can confidently derive the conclusion that these verses in Acts 16 refer to the Holy Spirit baptism. The last reference to baptism in Acts is the baptism of the disciples in Ephesus (Acts 19:1–7), and it is very clear that this baptism was of the Holy Spirit since Paul laid his hands on them.

In Paul's letter to the church in Ephesus, he encourages them to walk a life according to God's desires. His dissertation explains that there is a fleshly (desires of the world) way to walk versus the Holy Spirit's way. Paul understood that for believers to walk how God desires them to walk, they need to be influenced by the Holy Spirit. He uses an illustration that helps the reader understand that influence. "Do not get drunk with wine, for that is dissipation, but be filled with the Spirit" (Eph. 5:18). A person who has too much alcohol to drink to the point of being drunk has a mind that is compromised and impaired because of the chemical reaction in the brain. The legal term we use today for this condition is "being under the influence" (of alcohol). This is the same concept Paul had in mind when he contrasts the influence of wine with the Holy Spirit.

The Holy Spirit Baptism is receiving an influence that convicts us of sin, teaches us the truth of Jesus Christ, gives us a new life, directs our conduct toward holiness, confirms our inheritance as children of God, provides a direct line of communication to the Father, and instills us with unique gifts.

Fire Baptism

> *John answered and said to them all, "As for me, I baptize you with water; but One is coming who is mightier than I, and I am not fit to untie the thong of His sandals; He will baptize you with the Holy Spirit and fire."*
>
> —Luke 3:16

The fourth baptism is fire. In the Bible, fire is critical for all believers to understand and grasp. The Word of the Lord is filled with references and illustrations involving fire. It is used when describing the very presence and protection of God, the eradication of unrighteousness, and judgment. Throughout the Word of God, fire is an attention-getter. The Lord uses fire as a mysterious but deliberate mechanism that makes humanity take notice and pay attention to the events surrounding His display of power.

Fire is God's way of showing His presence to humanity, predominantly in the Old Testament. When God interacted with humanity, fire was commonly present. Revelations and visions to humans were accompanied with a form of fire that signifies the presence of God. The following recorded events of God's interaction with humanity have the common element of fire:

- In the covenant God made with Abraham, the presence of God was displayed by a flaming torch that passed between the halves of animals as His signature of commitment (Gen. 15:1–17).
- Moses experienced fire that did not consume a bush that was the presence of God (Exod. 3:1–6). One of the

plagues God sent against Egypt was hail and fire from heaven (Exod. 9:22–26). God led the nation of Israel with a pillar of fire (Exod. 13:21–22). God came down to Mount Sinai in the form of fire when Moses received the commandments directly from God (Exod. 19:16–20).

- God spoke to His people out of the midst of fire (Deut. 4:9–40; 5:4–5, 22–27; 9:10–15; 10:4–5). In Deuteronomy 18:15–22, a change occurs in the way God relates to humanity. The people requested to not deal with the fire of God anymore, and God agreed by putting in place the position of prophets who would receive commands and directions from God and relay them to the people.
- David equates the Lord's voice to a flaming fire (Ps. 29:7). The psalmist indicates that a consuming fire goes ahead of God (Ps. 50:1–4; 97:1–6).
- Isaiah relates fire to the presence of the Lord in Zion and Jerusalem (Isa. 31:9).
- Jeremiah says the words of God are like fire (Jer. 23:28–29).
- In Ezekiel's vision, preceding God was an enormous cloud and flashing fire (Ezek. 1:1–14). Within the cherubim, Ezekiel saw wheels of fire (Ezek. 10:1–8). The holy mountain contained stones of fire (Ezek. 28:11–19).
- Daniel's vision of the Ancient of Days (the Lord) describes His throne as ablaze, flowing with a river of fire (Dan. 7:1–10).
- Elijah was taken up to heaven in a fiery chariot pulled by fiery horses (2 Kings 2:11).
- In John's vision, when the seventh seal is broken, there is an angel who fills his golden censer with fire from the heavenly altar and throws it to the earth (Rev. 8:1–5).

All these supernatural events show us the power of God displayed through physical fire. The Bible tells us that fire is God's minister (also translated as *attendant, servant*) in Psalm 104:4 and Hebrews 1:7. God's use of fire represents His presence among humanity.

God's fire also is a display of His protection for His people. When the Arameans came to capture Elisha in Dothan, God opened their eyes to see horses and chariots of fire around Elisha (2 Kings 6:8–23). In Zechariah's vision, the future Jerusalem did not have physical walls because the Lord protected the city with a wall of fire (Zech. 1:18–2:5).

---

*God uses fire to display His powerful presence
and protection.*

Another use of fire by God is the eradication of sin from His people. Sin must be completely destroyed and eliminated forever. During the time of the Law (Old Testament), God used fire as the mechanism to annihilate sin into ashes. The following are recorded events where fire represents the eradication of sin.

- In the first eight chapters of Leviticus, the ordinances to eradicate sin and remain in a relationship with God incorporated fire to burn sacrifices.
- Leviticus 9 demonstrates that the human activity of burning sacrifices is deficient. In verse 24, after Moses and Aaron came out of the inner sanctuary, fire came out from the Holy of Holies where God resided and consumed the burnt offering.

- After Solomon completed building the temple and of-
  fered a prayer of consecration, "fire came down from
  heaven and consumed the burnt offering and the sacrifices, and the glory of the LORD filled the house" (2
  Chron. 7:1).
- When Isaiah saw the throne of the Lord, he was
  remorseful because his lips were contaminated with
  sin and incapable of speaking the words of God. The
  mechanism for administering forgiveness was a hot coal
  off heaven's altar (Isa. 6:1–8).

These are physical displays of what God's baptism of fire does
for us.

God's fire is the total eradication of sin.

The Lord used fire to consume His enemies and display
His wrath to the unrighteous. In Deuteronomy 4:15–24, Moses
warned the nation of Israel to never forget the covenant of the
Lord and to not worship anything but Him. Moses tells Israel that
God is a jealous God, and His form of discipline is a consuming
fire. This message is consistent throughout the Old Testament as
the references in the footnote explain.[10]

---

10. Psalm 11:5–6; 18:1–15; 21:7–11; 78:56–64; 104:1–4; Isaiah 26:7–11; 29:5–6;
30:27–31; 33:10–16; Jeremiah 4:3–4; 5:14–15; 6:27–30; 15:12–14; 17:1–4, 27;
21:11–12; 22:6–7; 43:8–13; 49:23–27; 50:29–32; 51:58; Lamentations 2:1–3;
11:11; Ezekiel 15:1–8; 20:43–49; 21:28–32; 22:17–31; 23:22–27; 24:1–13;
30:6–19; 36:4–5; 38:14–23; 39:1–6; Daniel 7:1–14; Hosea 8:11–14; Amos
1:1–2:5; Nahum 1:2–8; Zephaniah 1:14–18; 3:8–9.

The following are examples of how God judged evil with fire.

• Nadab and Abihu made the mistake of offering their own unauthorized version of sacrifice to the Lord (Lev. 10:1). God responds to their disobedience of not following His commands and ordinances. "And fire came out from the presence of the LORD and consumed them, and they died before the LORD" (Lev. 10:2).

• When the Lord heard Israel complaining, He angrily caused fire to consume some of the outer parts of their camp (Num. 11:1–3).

• Korah, Dathan, and Abiram rebelled against Moses and boldly took Moses up on a challenge to see who God appointed. In a showdown between Moses who had God and these three rebels who had a following of 250 men, the earth swallowed the rebels' families, and fire consumed the 250 men (Num. 16:1–35).

• As Israel was preparing to cross the Jordan River, their comfort was that the Lord went before them as a consuming fire to destroy the Anakites (Deut. 9:1–3).

• In a celebration of God's triumphs over Israel's enemies, David associated God's actions with a devouring fire from His mouth (2 Sam. 22:1–9).

• Elijah prevailed in his standoff with 450 prophets of Baal when God's fire consumed the Baal altars, including the offerings, wood, stone, dirt, and water (1 Kings 18:16–40).

• Ahaziah, who sought advice from Baal Zebub, twice sent a captain and 50 soldiers to retrieve Elijah, and both times, fire came down from the sky (from God) and consumed the captains and soldiers (2 Kings 1:1–18).

The Lord will judge all humanity with fire (Isa. 66:14–16). The final destiny of the unrighteous is the lake of fire, and their final judgment is to be cast into an eternal punishment of fire (Rev. 20:14–15).

God's fire is His device of judgment.

Fire is the presence and protection of God and the eradication of sin. Judgment is most likely what John understood when he stated, "I baptize you with water for repentance, but He who is coming after me is mightier than I, and I am not fit to remove His sandals; He will baptize you with the Holy Spirit and fire" (Matt. 3:11; also see Luke 3:16). John understood that Jesus's baptism was on a different level than his. John's baptism was a physical ritual around an earthly commodity of water, while Jesus's baptism was from heaven and the very throne room of the Father. It is something bigger, something more powerful, and something directly from the Creator that is administered to those who believe. Jesus immerses us into the presence and protection of the Holy God, eradicates our sins, and in the end will judge unrighteousness with fire.[11]

In Acts 2, Luke documents the physical display of fire baptism at Pentecost when the tongues of fire rested on the disciples as they were filled with the Holy Spirit. What occurred during this event was Jesus immersing the believers with the Holy Spirit and fire. This was a baptism of the personal indwelling of the presence of God and the eradication of sin, a phenomenon that was personal

---

11. Matthew 7:15–23; 13:36–50; 18:8–9; 25:31–46; Mark 9:42–49; Luke 3:7–9; 12:49; John 15:1–6; 2 Thessalonians 1:5–8; Hebrews 10:26–27; James 5:1–6; Revelation 19:19–21; 20:7–15; 21:6–8.

and spiritual. For the sake of those in attendance at Pentecost, God displayed a physical appearance of a spiritual function. Such a display was to guide the disciples in the transition from a physical, corporate, legalistic realm (sacrifices and water events) into a spiritual, individualistic grace era of the church.

Humanity's relationship with God is no longer conducted through visible buildings, altars, priests, or rituals. Today, our relationship with God is a personalized connection with direct spiritual access. Fire baptism by Jesus happens within each individual and is initiated by repentance. The forgiveness of sin occurs with a baptism that is administered through Jesus. The result of fire baptism is our sins being removed as far as the east is from the west (Ps. 103:9–12) and thrown into the depths of the sea (Micah 7:19).

Everyone will face the fire of the Lord at some point in time (Mark 9:49–50). The author of Hebrews reiterates that "our God is a consuming fire" (Heb. 12:29). We have a choice: repent and follow Jesus being baptized in His sin-eradicating fire or face Him at the final judgment that will lead to being thrown in the lake of fire. Unrighteousness cannot and will not exist in the presence of God; therefore, it will be completely eliminated. Jesus eliminates believers' unrighteousness so they can approach the throne of the Father, as the book of Hebrews teaches. Those resisting the baptism of fire in this life cannot enter heaven and will be sent to an eternal punishment of fire.

Fire baptism that Jesus brings to His followers is the presence and protection of God and the eradication of sin. For those who choose not to follow Him, fire baptism is judgment.

79

Blood Baptism

> *But Jesus said to them, "You do not know what you*
> *are asking. Are you able to drink the cup that I drink,*
> *or to be baptized with the baptism with which I am*
> *baptized?" They said to Him, "We are able." And*
> *Jesus said to them, "The cup that I drink you shall*
> *drink; and you shall be baptized with the baptism*
> *with which I am baptized."*
>
> —Mark 10:38–39

Blood baptism has two distinguishing aspects: salvation and suffering. Blood was essential to the sacrificial system that God put in place, described with great detail and precision in the first five books of the Bible. The association of blood to salvation was evident in the Passover event when the blood of the lamb was sprinkled on the doorposts, saving the lives of Israel's first-born sons (Exod. 12:1–29). Blood was used in the consecration (cleansing) of Aaron when he became the High Priest (Lev. 8:22–24). After receiving the ordinances from the Lord, Moses administrated a covenant with the people by sprinkling blood on them (Exod. 24:3–11). Blood must be shed to acquire the cleansing of sin and the receiving of salvation.

During James's and John's dialogue with Jesus about who would sit beside Him in heaven, Jesus asks them if they are able to drink the cup He drinks or be baptized with the baptism He experienced. Jesus was referring to baptism as His upcoming suffering, persecution, rejection, separation from the Father, and death on the cross (Luke 12:49–50). When James and John responded that they were able, Jesus replied, "The cup that I drink you shall drink; and you shall be baptized with the baptism with which I am baptized" (Mark 10:39). This is the baptism of the blood. Jesus baptizes us in His blood that He shed on the cross as a complete payment for our sins, providing us salvation.

Everyone who believes in the Messiah's sacrificial death is baptized in His blood of consecration and ushered into His New Covenant administration. We need to identify with Christ's work and grasp His sacrifice that took our penalty of sin and reconciled our position with the Holy Father. He did this by suffering through the separation from His Father for us. Romans 5:9–10 tells us that because of the blood of Christ, we are justified, reconciled, and saved. Because of our immersion in the blood of Jesus, we now have direct access to the holy sanctuary where the Father resides (Heb. 10:19–20).

In the best articulate language Paul could possibly use, he communicates this abstract concept of baptism in the blood of Christ.

What shall we say then? Are we to continue in sin so that grace may increase? May it never be! How shall we who died to sin still live in it? Or do you not know that all of us who have been baptized into Christ Jesus have been baptized into His death? Therefore, we have been buried with Him through baptism into death, so that as Christ was raised from the dead through the glory of the Father, so we too might walk in newness of life. For if we have become united with Him in the likeness of His death, certainly we shall also be in the likeness of His resurrection, knowing this, that our old self was crucified with Him, in order that our body of sin might be done away with, so that we would no longer be slaves to sin; for he who has died is freed from sin.

Now if we have died with Christ, we believe that we shall also live with Him, knowing that Christ, having been raised from the dead, is never to die again; death no longer is master over Him. For the death that He died, He died to sin once for all; but the life that He lives, He lives to God. Even so consider yourselves to be dead to sin, but alive to God in Christ Jesus.

—Rom. 6:1–11

We have participated in Christ's death. Our flesh (human sin nature) died with Jesus on the cross. Our sins died with the Messiah's last breath. Later in Romans, Paul tells us that the flesh needs to be put to death, and the Holy Spirit needs to dwell in us and live through us (Rom. 8:1–17). We are crucified with Christ; our old sin nature is killed, freeing us from sin and making us alive! We are alive in Christ, having a reconciled relationship with God the Father! That is the result of being flooded with the blood of Christ. The death of our flesh is the cup and baptism Christ referred to when he was talking to James and John.

Mainstream Christendom uses the verses in Romans 6 to support the earthly, physical water event. It teaches that the act of going under the water is a symbol of dying as the old self, and coming out of the water symbolizes resurrecting in a new life. Okay. That's wonderful symbolism. However, Christ did that for us when He died and was resurrected. In Romans 5:8–11, Paul writes that while we were still sinners (before we committed to follow Christ), He died for us, and we are justified and reconciled by His blood.

Douglas Moo in his commentary *The Epistle to the Romans* writes this about Romans 6:3–4:

> *The theology of this paragraph is both profound and controversial. What makes for the controversy are the related questions of the meaning and importance of baptism (vv. 3–4) and the relationship between baptism and the "with Christ" language. . . . Baptism is not the theme of the paragraph nor is it Paul's purpose to exposit his theology of baptism.* **Baptism, rather, functions as shorthand for the conversion experience as a whole.** *As such, it is the instrument (note the "through" in v. 4) by which we are put into relationship with the death and burial of Christ. It is not, then, that baptism is a symbol of dying and raising with Christ; nor is it that baptism is the place at which we die and rise with Christ. Dying and rising with Christ refers to the participation of the believer in the redemptive events themselves; and the ultimate basis for Paul's appeal in this chapter is not what happened when we were baptized, but what happened when Christ died and rose again* (emphasis added).[12]

The emphasized portion of this quote is a great statement that supports the word *baptism* as a broad and conceptual term. Moo defines very well that the term in the context of Romans 6 encompasses more than an earthly, water, symbolic action and rather the believer's redemption because of the action of Christ.

---

12. Douglas J. Moo, *The Epistle to the Romans* (Grand Rapids, MI: Wm. B. Eerdmans Publishing Co., 1996), 355.

It is a redemption that is the result of God's grace and love for humanity. True believers give up the right and privilege to follow the attractions of the world for following the righteousness that the Lord commands. Following the world is death; following the Lord is being raised to the heavens and eternal life.

Bultema quotes John Brown's position of baptism as stated in Romans 6:3–4. "The phrase 'baptized into Jesus Christ' occurs only here and in Galatians 3:27, and cannot be understood of the baptism by water."[13] Bultema's thesis in a chapter on baptism in Romans is that believers are not called to go down into the grave (referring to burial) but to raise up to the heavens (Eph. 2:6). His position of Romans 6 is that the concept of baptism is what Christ did through His death, burial, and resurrection, giving believers redemption, reconciliation, and new life.[14]

Romans 6:3–4 is about receiving the *Baptism of Grace*. When this is recognized, the true believer will change their lifestyle and follow the Lord (*Followship*). Unless we fully understand what the Lord did for us through His grace, we will never have the desire to deny the enticing worldly life and follow how He wants us to live. Because the Lord administers the *Baptism of Grace* on us, Paul tells us to kill the actions that cause eternal death and adopt the actions that provide eternal life.

Paul states that we were baptized into the Messiah's burial.

See to it that no one takes you captive through philosophy and empty deception, according to the tradition of men, according to the elementary principles

---

13. Harry Bultema, *The Bible and Baptism: A Re-Examination* (Muskegon, MI: Bultema Memorial Publication Society, 1955), 85–89.
14. Ibid.

of the world, rather than according to Christ. For in Him all the fullness of Deity dwells in bodily form, and in Him you have been made complete, and He is the head over all rule and authority; and in Him you were also circumcised with a circumcision made without hands, in the removal of the body of the flesh by the circumcision of Christ; having been buried with Him in baptism, in which you were also raised up with Him through faith in the working of God, who raised Him from the dead. When you were dead in your transgressions and the uncircumcision of your flesh, He made you alive together with Him, having forgiven us all our transgressions, having canceled out the certificate of debt consisting of decrees against us, which was hostile to us; and He has taken it out of the way, having nailed it to the cross.

—Col. 2:8–14

This passage in Colossians starts off with Paul warning his readers to not be deceived by philosophy and empty traditions of men. Then Paul makes the statement that we are completed in Christ. This completeness is obtained through the spiritual circumcision and baptism performed by the Messiah "with a circumcision made without hands." The removal of the default human sinfulness (flesh) and the subsequent consequences were performed when the Messiah took our sins on the cross. This is the spiritual circumcision. With the same thought process, Paul writes that we are immersed into the burial of the Messiah. The reference is not a physical function but a spiritual burial of our sin nature, and it is performed by the Messiah.

The sin nature leads to death, so it must be cut off and buried only to be renewed in a new life. Only because of the work done by Jesus can this new life be achieved. In Paul's writing to the Galatians against the Judaizers, he states that neither circumcision nor uncircumcision (physical) means anything (Gal. 5:1–6). The consistent message is that human-performed earthly, physical actions are meaningless because of Christ's work that replaces all physical requirements.

Hebrews tells us that Jesus is the forever High Priest who "has taken His seat" at the right hand of the Father (Heb. 8:1–2). His work is done. The physical requirement is over. When Jesus gave Himself up as the ultimate sacrifice, He paid the debt of punishment, spiritually circumcised our sins, and regenerated us to a new life. First John 1:7–9 confirms that our responsibility is to acknowledge that we sin by failing to live up to God's standards. When we recognize this sin and understand that it is the wedge that separates us from God the Father, we then have a responsibility to own up to it and communicate our remorse for our failures to the Father. By taking this action of repentance, God the Father then does all the work. He forgives and cleanses us. He does that through the cleansing blood of Jesus His Son. Jesus did the work, and there is nothing physical we can do to gain, add to, or receive salvation. Repentance is the only action required.

Because of Christ's work, we are complete and alive. The fleshly body (sin nature) is cut off and buried with Him, and we have been raised with Him into a new life, forgiven of all our failures.

Therefore if you have been raised up with Christ, keep seeking the things above, where Christ is, seated at the right hand of God. Set your mind on the things above, not on the things that are on earth. For you

*have died and your life is hidden with Christ in God.
When Christ, who is our life, is revealed, then you
also will be revealed with Him in glory.*

—Col. 3:1–4

The baptism in Mark 10:38–39 refers to what Christ did for us through His death, burial, and resurrection. Our responsibility is to recognize the Messiah's sacrifice on the cross, admit our failures, commit to associate with His death, accept what He has done for us, and choose to follow the Holy Spirit's influence in our lives. That is when we are submerged in the Messiah's saving blood.

---

*Jesus immerses us in His blood,
which cleanses our sins and gives us salvation.*

The second element of the blood baptism is unpopular among many Christians today. It is the baptism of suffering. When we become a follower of Christ and are baptized with His baptism, it includes becoming an enemy of the world. When we commit our allegiance to Christ, we commit treason against satan, the ruler of this physical earth.[15] Jesus told His disciples and us in John 15:18–19 that the world hates us because we are not of the world. Paul's life example was one of suffering and being persecuted for

---

15. A world whose god and ruler is satan: 2 Corinthians 4:4, god of this age. We live in a period of evil: Galatians 1:3–5, present evil age. A period of spiritual darkness and evil: Ephesians 6:12, powers of this dark world, forces of evil. This world produces its own wisdom out of the darkness: 1 Corinthians 2:6–8, wisdom of this age or of the rulers of this age. Predominant today is ungodliness and lust: Titus 2:11–14, ungodliness and worldly passions. There is a world pattern different than God's desire: Romans 12:1–2, the pattern of this world. This world is ruled by the spirit of sinful craving: Ephesians 2:1–3, ways of this world and of the ruler of the kingdom of the air, the spirit who is now at work in those who are disobedient.

the cause of Christ. In his second letter to Timothy, he writes that "all who desire to live godly in Christ Jesus will be persecuted" (2 Tim. 3:12). This topic does not make a book a top seller nor will it break records on a social media hit list. But it is the reality of the Christian life. The encouragement from Paul's report is that "out of them all [sufferings] the Lord rescued me!" (2 Tim. 3:11). We have a hope in Paul's testimony that God rescues us out of our suffering.

Peter's first letter to the Gentiles is an encouragement to persevere through suffering. He encourages his readers to conduct themselves during their time on earth worthy of the honor of being baptized in the precious blood of Christ (1 Pet. 1:18–21). Later in the letter, Peter challenges the readers to endure through suffering of false accusations just as Jesus did by dying on the cross (1 Pet. 2:20–25).

Peter continues in 1 Peter 3:13–22 with a charge to withstand criticism and ridicule. He uses the example of Noah when he was building the ark. Noah's being saved through the water is the illustration Peter uses to explain how perseverance of faith through persecution ultimately results in God doing what He promised and saving us. In the context of Peter's writing, baptism here is the baptism of suffering just as Noah was ridiculed and Jesus also suffered. The baptism in this text is the baptism of suffering. Jesus told the disciples that they would be baptized with His suffering blood. Peter's thesis is to remain faithful in obedience while the world attacks and condemns our allegiance to Christ.

Just like Paul and Noah, the baptism of suffering increases our faith and trust in the Lord who will always rescue us!

Faithfulness and trust in the Lord through
persecution and suffering solidify our salvation.

Grace

The five baptisms found in the Bible are dispensed onto humanity by God the Father through the work of His Son. Living water is poured on us, giving us eternal life. The fullness of the three-person Godhead is revealed to us, giving us understanding. The Holy Spirit's influence encapsulates us, providing guidance and comfort. God's fire engulfs us, showing His presence, providing protection, and incinerating our sin. The blood of Christ covers us with salvation but also warns us that those who follow Him will be persecuted by the world.

When we believe that Jesus is the Son of God who died for our sins, was buried, rose from the dead, and now sits at the right hand of the Father, all five of these baptisms are poured onto and into our lives. There, then, is the reconciliation back into a relationship with the Father. He welcomes us into the family as His children with a promised inheritance that is sealed by the presence of the Holy Spirit in our lives. Because of God's love and grace, along with the work of the Messiah, we obtain the status of God's children through the one pure baptism (Eph. 4:5). This baptism is from the Father and includes all five aspects of the living water, the Trinity, the Holy Spirit, fire, and blood.

Grace is the loyal, loving favor God displays to humanity. All humanity is born in sin, which means our default conduct is to operate against God's laws and desires. Because God loves the humanity He created in His own image, He favors everyone. That is why Paul writes in Romans 5:8, "God demonstrates His own love toward us, in that while we were yet sinners, Christ died for us." In John 3:16, Jesus tells Nicodemus that "God so loved the world, that He gave His only begotten Son, that whoever believes in Him shall not perish but have eternal life." This is God's grace toward humanity. As rebellious as we are, as hard as we try to resist how He wants us to act and how fast we concede to temptation, God loves us even before we recognize that we need to admit our need for His forgiveness. Everyone, all humanity, every person who has lived, is living, and will live is covered under God's grace. First Timothy 2:4 tells us that God "desires all men to be saved and to come to the knowledge of the truth." God's grace is not limited to a select few.

By studying the Old Testament, we see God's grace as He continually motivates, disciplines, challenges, and warns the nation of Israel to return and worship Him and Him alone. He shows great patience and restraint with a rebellious and adulterous people who forgot Him and lived satisfying their own desires. Even when God punished the nation, He showed His grace by retaining a remnant of the nation whose descendents would produce His promised, forever-reigning King. He then provides the most significant statement of grace in the form of this descendent, His Son, the Messiah.

Salvation through Jesus Christ is available for all people—it is for everyone. It is for every sinner. It is for every nationality, every economic status, every mental capacity, every gender, and every age. This is the unlimited grace element of God, and because of His love, He provided a solution to our depravity, allowing us to unite with Him and become His children. Romans 6:23 tells us that God gives us the gift of salvation and that life with Him is free. Ephesians 2:8 explains that we are saved by grace through faith in Him. First John 1:9 promises that if we confess our sins, He will forgive us and completely cleanse us of our sins. God's grace is free and obtainable through faith alone. Period.

Grace is a dominant characteristic of God. Charles R. Swindoll in his book *The Grace Awakening* says that "to show grace is to extend favor or kindness to one who doesn't deserve it and can never earn it."[1] Swindoll explains that the Hebrew concept of grace is "to bend; to stoop." The concept is when someone in royalty stops and kneels to address a common person.[2] This displays a picture of God lowering Himself to humanity's level in an action of showing us how valuable we are to Him. God displayed grace when He sent His Son to humanity and absorbed the penalty of sin.

Philip Yancey, even though he laments that he has trouble defining grace, does a masterful job with these two statements: "Grace means there is nothing we can do to make God love us more. And grace means there is nothing we can do to make God love us less."[3] Grace is God displaying His love to us.

Gematria is a numerical system where each letter corresponds to a number value in the Hebrew language. Using the

1. Charles R. Swindoll, *The Grace Awakening* (Dallas, TX: Word Publishing, 1996), 9.
2. Ibid.
3. Philip Yancey, *What's So Amazing about Grace?* (Grand Rapids, MI: Zondervan Publishing, 1997), 70.

Gematria system, the two letters for grace, חן, total the value of the number five. Five is the representation of the grace of God. Multiples of five represent grace upon grace. The number five is evident throughout the Word of God and is used strategically where God displays His grace to His people. Here are some examples of how the Lord represents His grace using five and multiples of five.[4]

God instituted five offerings that the nation of Israel brought before Him.

1. Burnt: Leviticus 1; 8:18–21; 16:3, 24
2. Sin: Leviticus 4; 16:3–22
3. Guilt: Leviticus 5:14–19; 6:1–7; 7:1–7
4. Grain: Leviticus 2
5. Peace: Leviticus 3; 7:11–34

The Law is contained in the first five books of the Bible, called the Pentateuch.

The tabernacle's structure was built with a variation of five components and measures.

> Five curtains: Exodus 26:3
> Five bars: Exodus 26:26–27
> Five pillars and socket: Exodus 26:37
> Bronze altar (five cubits long and wide): Exodus 27:1
> Court size (100 cubits long, 50 cubits wide, 5 cubits high): Exodus 27:18

---

4. The following websites define the meaning of the number five: http://www.biblestudy.org/bibleref/meaning-of-numbers-in-bible/5.html, http://www.agapebiblestudy.com/documents/The%20Significance%20of%20Numbers%20in%20Scripture.htm.

The holy anointing oil is made up of five ingredients (Exod. 30:23–24).

> 500 shekels of myrrh
> 250 shekels of cinnamon
> 250 shekels of cane
> 500 of cassia
> Hin of olive oil

When David faced Goliath, he gathered five smooth stones (1 Sam. 17:40).

Solomon's temple was built with a variation of five components and measures.

> Entrance doorpost of the inner sanctuary was five-sided (1 Kings 6:31).
> Cherubim wing length in the holy of holies was five cubits (2 Chron. 3:10–13)
> Ten wash basins (five on left and five on right) (2 Chron. 4:6)
> Ten golden lampstands (five on left and five on right) (2 Chron. 4:7)
> Ten tables (five on left and five on right) (2 Chron. 4:8)

Jubilee year: 50th year

> The year of emancipation and restoration (Lev. 25)

Pentecost: 50th day

> 50 days after Passover
> Count started the day after the Sabbath (resurrection day)
> Number meaning jubilee
> Feast of Weeks (Exod. 34:22)
> Holy Spirit's descension (Acts 2:1)

The fivefold baptism is God's display of grace onto the believer. He immerses us into the living water of eternal life. He overwhelms us with the knowledge of God in three persons, displaying an incomprehensible love. He influences us with His Spirit who guides, corrects, and comforts. He purifies us with fire that eradicates our sins. He washes us with His cleansing blood that perfects us.

The one baptism referenced in Ephesians 4:5 is the Lord immersing believers in the *Baptism of Grace* and supersaturating them with His loving grace. Paul's communication on this concept of God baptizing us with His grace is expressed with statements such as "He freely bestowed on us" (Eph. 1:6), "He lavished on us" (Eph. 1:8), "He might show the surpassing riches" (Eph. 2:7), "the surpassing grace of God in you," (2 Cor. 9:14), "God set me apart . . . called me" (Gal. 1:15), and "was more than abundant" (1 Tim. 1:14).

Peter also communicates the *Baptism of Grace* concept with the expression "be multiplied to you" (2 Pet. 1:2).

James states that God gives greater grace to the humble (James 4:5–6).

Strong's Concordance defines grace as "the merciful kindness by which God, exerting his holy influence upon souls, turns them to Christ, keeps, strengthens, increases them in Christian faith, knowledge, affection, and kindles them to the exercise of the Christian virtues."[5] The implication is that God's grace is continuous. Not only does His grace provide salvation, but it is also the ongoing force that builds our relationship with the Father.

---

5. *Lumina,* https://netbible.org/bible/Ephesians+2, Ephesians 2:8, Greek translation, Grace. Taken from NET Bible® copyright ©1996, 2019 by Biblical Studies Press, L.L.C. http://netbible.com. All rights reserved.

God covers us with His grace—a grace that is beyond our understanding, a grace that cannot be earned, a grace that is not generated by human action or ritual, a grace that forgives the grossest offence. It is a grace where a liar, adulterer, and murderer (David) is called a man after God's own heart. It is a grace where a destroyer of the church (Paul) is changed into a great preacher, missionary, and advocate. It is a grace where a denier (Peter) is commissioned to disciple God's people. It is a grace for all of us that is far greater than any of our failures. God provides this grace through His Son's purifying blood and fire, His fullness incorporated in our lives, eternal life from the living water, all made aware to us through His guiding Spirit.

Our job is to believe and have faith. The work of our salvation is all done by the Lord!

The Lord receives all the credit for the work accomplished in us through His *Baptism of Grace*. When we understand what the Lord has done and that He is the instituter of baptism, we will only boast about His work as Paul instructs in 2 Corinthians 10:12–18 and as recorded in Jeremiah.

> *Thus says the LORD, "Let not a wise man boast of his wisdom, and let not the mighty man boast of his might, let not a rich man boast of his riches; but let him who boasts boast of this, that he understands and knows Me, that I am the LORD who exercises lovingkindness, justice and righteousness on earth; for I delight in these things," declares the LORD.*
> —Jer. 9:23–24

Conclusion

When reading the words *baptize* and *baptism* in the Bible, we must be diligent to remain true to the author's intended message. The reader's understanding of the terms used by the author must match the context of the author's complete message. Approaching the Bible should be the same as approaching any literature by utilizing the context to help define words within the text. Not only does the immediate context need to be understood, but we must also understand the message of the whole document or letter the author wrote, as well as the teachings and truths throughout the Bible. When the word *baptism* is used, the reader needs to guard against thinking it refers to the current culture-dominated definition of only an earthly, physical water event. Here is a question to ask: What is the message the author is presenting, and how does the word *baptism* help illustrate or define the main point?

With a comprehension of the fullness, beauty, and magnitude of God's *Baptism of Grace*, Scripture becomes clearer and makes more logical sense. By changing our thoughts when we read the word *baptism* from an earthly, physical action to inserting one or more or all five forms of baptism into the contextual writing, God's grace becomes apparent, and the author's intent is better comprehended.

Immersion of living water that comes from the heavenly throne, faith and belief in the Triune God, a life influenced by the Holy Spirit's guidance, fiery forgiveness of sins, and the conjoining in the flesh's crucifixion through the cleansing blood of Christ all culminate in our salvation. To receive this baptism, the action is the same as it has been throughout history like it was during the sacrifice era before Christ and during John the Baptizer's water event. The action is repentance! We must recognize that we are unrighteous and that our only recourse for forgiveness is to admit our faults and confess that our salvation from the fiery judgment is by believing in Jesus Christ who paid the debt for us.

Once we choose to believe and have faith in the saving grace of the Father, we obtain eternal life, gain knowledge and understanding of the Godhead, are submersed with the Holy Spirit's leading, and forgiven of all sin. Our lives are changed. God then views us as righteous. We choose to repent, believe, and have faith. God immerses us into a spotless life where sin is forgiven and forgotten, allowing us direct access to the throne of the Father. It is then that we abide eternally as His children. The Holy Spirit becomes our daily influential guide as we live on this earth striving for righteousness and obedience. God does the work as we receive the blessing of His *Baptism of Grace*.

The second chapter of Acts (specifically verse 38) is a flagship text used to support the action of baptism. There are many propositions and writings that use this text to support various positions regarding the mode, need, and requirement of baptism for salvation. Let's look at the first question we need to address.

Was there water involved in this event? Another challenging question is this: How is it physically possible for 3,000 people to be baptized in one day? There are many rationalizations that have been formulated to answer these questions, but none of them can be substantiated; they only rest on speculation and assumptions. The translation notes from the New English Translation Bible (see footnote) identify four positions derived from this text.[1] If the baptism in Acts 2:38 is the *Baptism of Grace*, then the controversy goes away. The questions are answered because the Lord does the baptizing with the all-encompassing saving action of His grace.

---

1. *Lumina*, Translation note on Acts 2:38, https://netbible.org/bible/Acts+2 There is debate over the meaning of εἰς in the prepositional phrase εἰς ἄφεσιν τῶν ἁμαρτιῶν ὑμῶν (east aphesin tōn hamartiōn hummin, "for/ because of/with reference to the forgiveness of your sins"). Although a causal sense has been argued, it is difficult to maintain here. *Elsy* 369-71 discusses at least four other ways of dealing with the passage: (1) The baptism referred to here is physical only, and εἰς has the meaning of "for" or "unto." Such a view suggests that salvation is based on works—an idea that runs counter to the theology of Acts, namely: (a) repentance often precedes baptism (cf. Acts 3:19; 26:20), and (b) salvation is entirely a gift of God, not procured via water baptism (Acts 10:43 [cf. v. 47]; 13:38-39, 48; 15:11; 16:30-31; 20:21; 26:18); (2) The baptism referred to here is spiritual only. Although such a view fits well with the theology of Acts, it does not fit well with the obvious meaning of "baptism" in Acts—especially in this text (cf. 2:41); (3) The text should be repunctuated in light of the shift from second person plural to third person singular back to second person plural again. The idea then would be, "Repent *for/with reference to* your sins, and let each one of you be baptized . . ." Such a view is an acceptable way of handling εἰς, but its subtlety and awkwardness count against it; (4) Finally, it is possible that to a first-century Jewish audience (as well as to Peter), the idea of baptism might incorporate both the spiritual reality and the physical symbol. That Peter connects both closely in his thinking is clear from other passages such as Acts 10:47 and 11:15-16. If this interpretation is correct, then Acts 2:38 is saying very little about the specific theological relationship between the symbol and the reality, only that historically they were viewed together. Taken from NET Bible® copyright ©1996, 2019 by Biblical Studies Press, L.L.C. http://netbible.com. All rights reserved.

Using the *Baptism of Grace* concept helps us better understand Paul's statements that there is one baptism (1 Cor. 12:13; Eph. 2:14–18; 4:3–5). Refreshed by the living water, adopted by the three-person God, being controlled by the Holy Spirit, being forgiven of sins and regenerated to a new person is the only saving baptism, and it is administered solely by the Lord. The method of this baptism is solely God's responsibility, thus eliminating any need for a human doctrinal position on how it is administered. Humanity's responsibility is to teach the truths of God's Word and make disciples. Jesus does the saving and baptizing.

The *Baptism of Grace* helps us better understand the challenging and controversial text in 1 John where the Apostle John expounds on this concept by indicating that Jesus came by water and blood.

This is the One who came by water and blood, Jesus Christ; not with the water only, but with the water and with the blood. It is the Spirit who testifies, because the Spirit is the truth. For there are three that testify: the Spirit and the water and the blood; and the three are in agreement. If we receive the testimony of men, the testimony of God is greater; for the testimony of God is this, that He has testified concerning His Son. The one who believes in the Son of God has the testimony in himself; the one who does not believe God has made Him a liar, because he has not believed in the testimony that God has given concerning His Son. And the testimony is this, that God has given us eternal life, and this life is in His Son. He who has the Son has the life; he who does not have the Son of God does not have the life.

—1 John 5:6–12

Being consistent with John's references to the living water originating from the Father, Jesus came by the Father. Jesus is deity from Yahweh (God the Father) who was born a human in bodily form that consists of blood. Being from the living water and taking on the form of man testifies that Jesus is Messiah who takes away the sin of the world and provides salvation to all who choose to believe in Him. The Holy Spirit is in full agreement with who the Messiah is and promotes His legacy as the Savior of the world. The Lord saves us through the eternal water and cleansing blood, and seals us with the Holy Spirit.

---

*How do we then deal with modern
Christendom where the earthly, physical water
act is so predominant and is espoused as the
primary doctrine of initiation for entry
into the kingdom?*

A Challenge

An adjustment in perspective is required. A reevaluation must be performed that honestly asks this question: Is a physical water act required? Before that question is answered, stop. Do not quote the "company line," but study the depth of God's Word, His grace, and what it really teaches. When you put aside all preconceived opinions, thoughts, and doctrines, you will find that God wants an individual relationship, not a human-developed, dictated, ritual-based relationship. In Mark 7:5–8, Jesus quotes the prophecy of Isaiah 29:13 and condemns holding human-developed traditions above the true teaching of God's Word. Jesus tells the Pharisees and scribes that they are more interested in tradition than they are in adhering to God's commands. The command for us today is simple but complex: love God and love people (Matt. 22:37–39). It's simple because there are no mandatory rituals involved. It's complex because every action, thought, and desire are measured against a love for the Creator and a love for everyone we encounter, with no exceptions.

The work the Lord does in each person is unique. Peter was directly called by Jesus, Paul was knocked off his horse, the centurion with a sick daughter approached Jesus, and the woman at the well was going about her daily task when Jesus started a conversation. Each encounter was unique. Our encounter with Jesus is also unique. Everyone's story is a unique testimony of how the Lord was revealed with the choice to follow Him or not.

The *Baptism of Grace* is a dynamic journey toward righteousness. That journey takes us through a refining process of sanctification (Rom. 6:19–23; I Thess. 4:3–7; 2 Thess. 2:13; Heb. 12:7–17). Jesus uses His fire to refine us through trials and tests (1 Pet. 1:3–12). In Deuteronomy 13:1–5, Moses documented that false prophets and false teachers will attempt to entice us to follow other gods and false teachings. Moses tells the people that they shall not listen to the false prophets or teachings and that God uses them as a test. Moses ends with a command, "You shall follow the LORD your God and fear Him; and you shall keep His commandments, listen to His voice, serve Him, and cling to Him . . . you shall purge the evil from among you" (Deut. 13:4–5). Today, Christians are fed false teachings regarding baptism. It is one of the idolatrous teachings in our cultural Christian church institutions. The teaching of baptism is the church institution's self-serving mechanism to hold people in captivity and require an act to be saved or join a denominational sect of people.

The teaching that an earthly, physical water baptism act is required must be purged from the assembly of people who follow the Lord and the truth of His Word.

Proposal

If an individual is convicted by the Lord (not denominational or religious pressure) that they need to perform the physical water event, then they had better do it. But if that conviction does not exist, then religious institutions must accept that the physical event is neither a requirement nor necessary for salvation and following the Lord.

We need to treat physical water baptism as an individual preference and choice. Eliminate any legalistic platforms, and embrace each other's individualism in the Spirit. We should rejoice when we encounter a person who is at peace with their walk and security with God, regardless of what rituals they participated in. Who are we as humans to instill stipulations when Paul tells us we are free in Christ?

This is a charge to approach the topic of baptism with openness and willingness to allow the Spirit of God to work in people's lives. This is a challenge to accept people for who they are in the Spirit and resist attempting to change them to fit a mold that only satisfies a human-developed requirement. We need to step out and do the hard work of discipling people. We need to understand where they are in their relationship with Christ and learn how the Spirit is working in their lives. When we make this investment, only then can we counsel people on how to address the topic of baptism.

Final Thoughts

Paul challenges the believers in Galatia regarding the false teachings that required them to adhere to an earthly, physical act of circumcision. In Galatians 3:2, Paul asks them a rhetorical question: "Did you receive the Spirit by works of the Law or by hearing with faith?"

Today we must answer the same question. Did you receive the Spirit by the works of an earthly, physical water act under the law or by faith?

Paul continues his postulation to the believers in Galatia in Galatians 5:1-6 by telling them that they are giving up their freedom by participating in the earthly, physical ritual of circumcision. His bold statement is that if they participated in circumcision, then "Christ will be of no benefit" (Gal. 5:2). Today, the participation of an earthly, physical water activity as a required act renders Christ worthless. The requirement of an earthly, physical water event, labeled baptism by mainstream church institutions, makes the work of Christ meaningless. It conveys that the freedom Christ provided through His sacrifice on the cross is not enough, and we need to add a ritual for our salvation or acceptance into the family.

Requiring an earthly physical water event must be reevaluated by God's people.

The church of Corinth was experiencing differences of opinion and internal quarreling. Paul then writes them a letter to address their issues and help set them straight. In 1 Corinthians 1:10-17,

Paul addresses that they are divided on the topic of baptism. Paul asks, "Has Christ been divided?" (1 Cor. 1:13). What a wake-up call! That is the same question Christendom needs to ask today. Paul goes on to say that the physical is not important and that his mission was not to baptize but to preach the gospel so the cross of Christ would not become void.

Today, we need to preach the gospel—period—so we do not nullify the cross of Christ.

The topic of baptism creates many questions that we have discussed in detail. Below is a chart with the most logical answers to these questions.

Question	Answer
What is the one baptism?	The *Baptism of Grace* from God (Eph. 4:5; 1 Cor. 12:13)
What is the proper method of baptism?	The *Baptism of Grace* from God (1 Cor. 6:11)
How are we saved?	By the *Baptism of Grace* from God (Titus 3:5–6)
Is baptism from humans or heaven?	The *Baptism of Grace* is from God in heaven (John 3:27)
How are we cleansed into righteousness?	By the *Baptism of Grace* from God (Heb. 10:19–22; Ps. 51; Ezek. 16:9)
What must we do?	Believe and have faith in God's supersaturating *Baptism of Grace* (Acts 2:21; 4:12; 15:11; 16:13; Rom. 10:13; Eph. 2:8–9)

The Lord instills upon you the *Baptism of Grace.* The saving grace of the Father is lavishly poured upon you as He immerses you in Himself, eliminates your sin, and guides you through this life in anticipation of living with Him in eternity.

May you have the freedom of His grace without any physical requirements.

May you follow the Lord and not earthly, human-made rituals and concepts.

May the Lord give you clarity, discernment, and exposure to the truth.

May the Lord give you wisdom as you process His *Baptism of Grace.*

Appendix:
Definition of Baptism
Research Notes

Vines Expository Dictionary—three variations of the root Greek word:

1. *baptisma* (a noun); the process of immersion, submersion, and emergence
2. *baptizo* (a verb) from the root *bapto*; to dip
3. *baptismos* (a noun); a ceremonial washing[1]

---

1. W. E. Vine, "An Expository Dictionary of New Testament Words with their Precise Meanings for English Readers," In W. E. Vine, *Vine's Complete Expository Dictionary of Old and New Testament Words* (Nashville, TN: Thomas Nelson, 1984), baptism, Baptist, baptize, 50.

Webster's Dictionary:

1. *baptize*; to immerse (an individual) in water, or pour, or sprinkle water over (the individual), as a symbol of admission into Christianity or a specific Christian church
2. *baptism*; the ceremony or sacrament of admitting a person into Christianity or a Christian church by immersing the individual in water or by pouring or sprinkling water on the individual, as a symbol of washing away sin and of spiritual purification[2]

The Tyndale Bible Dictionary:

Baptism: "to dip" or "immerse." It also describes the activity as the religious rite of initiation into the Christian community.[3]

Charles R. Swindoll and Roy B. Zuck—*Understanding Christian Theology*:

Baptize: "to immerse."[4]

James Wilkinson Dale (1812–1881)—*Classic Baptism*, 1867:

Argues that the definitions of *baptize* and *baptism* are not interchangeable. He also concludes that each term has a primary and secondary definition.

2. Victoria Neufeldt, and David B. Guralnik, eds. *Webster's New World Dictionary*, baptism, baptize, 109.
3. Walter A. Elwell, and Philip W. Comfort, eds., *Tyndale Bible Dictionary*. (Wheaton, IL: Tyndale House, 2001), baptism, 144–145.
4. Charles R. Swindoll, and Roy B. Zuck, eds., *Understanding Christian Theology* (Nashville, TN: Thomas Nelson, 2003), 1152.

1. Bapto, in primary use, expresses a definite act, characterized by various and essential limitations, to dip.
2. Bapto, dip, in secondary use, expresses a limited force, with a correspondingly limited effect.
3. Baptizo, in primary use, expresses condition, intusposition, without limitations.
4. Baptizo, in secondary use, expresses condition effected by controlling influence, without limitation of intusposition, or otherwise.[5]

Forty Greek uses of baptism:

1. to assault; 2. to let fall; 3. to flow; 4. to weigh down; 5. to walk; 6. to pierce; 7. to hurl down; 8. to march; 9. to rush down; 10. to surround; 11. to press down; 12. to rise above; 13. to dip; 14. to submerge; 15. to thrust; 16. to blow; 17. to rush down [sic]; 18. to strike; 19. to proceed; 20. to plunge; 21. to immerge; 22. to imbathe; 23. to plunge; 24. to lower down; 25. to immerse; 26. to come on; 27. to overturn; 28. to boil up; 29. to flood; 30. to whelm; 31. to let down; 32. to enter in; 33. to pour; 34. to souse; 35. to bring down; 36. to depress; 37. to steep; 38. to drench; 39. to play the dipping match; 40. to duck[6]

---

5. James W. Dale, *Classic Baptism: An Inquiry into the Meaning of the Word Baptizo as Determined by the Usage of Classical Greek Writers* (Boston: Draper & Halliday, 1867), 4–5.
6. Ibid., 74.

"To baptize—After a thoughtful consideration of every, apparently, appropriate word, I am induced to believe that it would be well employed baptize to represent the secondary use, defining it as expressing controlling influence; the particular nature of the influence being determined by the specialty of the case."

"I would define βαπτιζω to mean, primarily,

1. To INTUSPOSE: to merse, to drown, to whelm, to steep, to inn; and, by appropriation, *to suffocate within a fluid*, (to drown).
2. To INFLUENCE CONTROLLINGLY: to merse, to whelm, to steep, to inn, to baptize; and, by appropriation, *to intoxicate.*"

"Each of these words expresses a condition induced by some controlling influence."[7]

George Junkin, D.D.—One baptism as found in the Bible:

Baptism is "overwhelm" – pouring – not dipping[8]

Milo P. Jewett, A.M.—*The Mode and Subjects of Baptism*:

Jewett was a Presbyterian minister who changed his position of believing the proper mode of baptism is sprinkling

7. James W. Dale, *Classic Baptism; An Inquiry into the Meaning of the Word as Determined by the Usage of Classical Greek Writers* (Boston: Draper & Halliday, 1867), 134–135.
8. George D. Junkin, *One Baptism as Found in the Bible* (Philadelphia: Presbyterian Board of Publication and Sabbath-School Work, 1917).

to immersion and the recipient has to be one who believes versus infant baptism.[9]

John H. Godwin—*Christian Baptism*:

Βαπτίζω: to purify, purification[10]

John Stockton Axtell—*The Mystery of Baptism*:

Baptism is a ceremony – to dip[11]

Alexander Carson—*Baptism: Its Mode and Subjects*:

Bapto – it always signifies to dip; never expressing anything but mode.

Bapto and Baptizo have one signification no secondary meaning.[12]

Harry Bultema—*The Bible and Baptism: A Re-Examination*:

Baptizo – submerging so as to never to emerge[13]

---

9. Milo P. Jewett, *The Mode and Subjects of Baptism* (Boston: Gould, Kendall, and Lincoln, 1846).
10. John H. Godwin, *Christian Baptism. An Inquiry into the Scripture Evidence of Its Nature, the Mode, Subjects, and Design of the Rite, and the Meaning of the Term* (London: W. Blanchard and Sons, 1845).
11. John Stockton Axtell, *Mystery of Baptism* (New York: Funk & Wagnalls, 1901).
12. Alexander Carson, *Baptism: Its Mode and Subjects, Fifth Edition* (Grand Rapids, MI: Kregel Publications, 1981), 55.
13. Harry Bultema, *The Bible and Baptism: A Re-Examination* (Muskegon, MI: Bultema Memorial Publication Society, 1955), 19.

References

Axtell, John Stockton. *The Mystery of Baptism*. New York: Funk & Wagnalls, 1901.

Bultema, Harry. *The Bible and Baptism: A Re-Examination*. Muskegon, MI: Bultema Memorial Publication Society, 1955.

Carson, Alexander. *Baptism: Its Mode and Subjects, Fifth Edition*. Grand Rapids, MI: Kregel Publications, 1981.

Clowney, Edmund P. *The Church*. Downers Grove, IL: InterVarsity Press, 1995.

Constable, Thomas L. "Welcome to Sonic Light." https://planobiblechapel.org/soniclight/.

Conybeare, F. C. *History of New Testament Criticism*. New York: The Knickerbocker Press, 1910.

Dale, James W. *Classic Baptism; An Inquiry into the Meaning of the Word Baptizo as Determined by the Usage of Classical Greek Writers*. Boston: Draper & Halliday, 1867.

"Does Matthew 28:19 Have Added Text?" Trinity Truth. https://www.trinitytruth.org/matthew28_19addedtext.html.

Elwell, Walter A., and Philip W. Comfort, eds. *Tyndale Bible Dictionary*. Wheaton, IL: Tyndale House Publisher, 2001.

Godwin, John H. *Christian Baptism: An Inquiry into the Scripture Evidence of Its Nature, the Mode, Subjects, and Design of the Rite, and the Meaning of the Term.* London: W. Blanchard and Sons, 1845.

González, Justo L. *The Story of Christianity.* New York: HarperCollins Publishers, 1984.

—. *The Story of Christianity.* New York: HarperCollins Publishers, 1985.

Jewett, Milo P., *The Mode and Subjects of Baptism.* Boston: Gould, Kendall, and Lincoln, 1846.

Junkin, George D. *One Baptism as Found in the Bible.* Philadelphia: Presbyterian Board of Publication and Sabbath-School Work, 1917.

Leith, John H. ed. *Creeds of the Churches.* Louisville, KY: John Knox Press, 1982.

Moo, Douglas J. *The Epistle to the Romans. New International Commentary on the New Testament.* Grand Rapids, MI: Wm. B. Eerdmans Publishing Co., 1996.

Morford, William J. *One New Man Bible: Revealing Jewish Roots and Power.* Travelers Rest, SC: True Potential Publishing, 2011.

The NET Bible, New English Translation. Biblical Study Press, 1996.

Neufeldt, Victoria, and David B. Guralnik, eds. *Webster's New World Dictionary of American English.* New York: Simon and Schuster, 1988.

Swindoll, Charles R. *The Grace Awakening*. Dallas: Word Publishing, 1996.

Swindoll, Charles R., and Roy B. Zuck, eds. *Understanding Christian Theology*. Nashville, TN: Thomas Nelson Publishers, 2003.

"Tertullian's Homily on Baptism." http://www.tertullian.org/articles/evans_bapt/evans_bapt_index.htm.

Vine, W. E. "An Expository Dictionary of New Testament Words with their Precise Meanings for English Readers." In W. E. Vine, ed. *Vine's Complete Expository Dictionary of Old and New Testament Words*. Nashville, TN: Thomas Nelson, 1984.

World Council of Churches. "Baptism, Eucharist, and Ministry: Commission on Faith and Order World Council of Churches." In John H. Leith, ed. *Creeds of the Churches*. Louisville, KY: John Knox Press, 1982.

Yancey, Philip. *What's So Amazing about Grace?* Grand Rapids, MI: Zondervan Publishing, 1997.